EVERY DAY GOD

heart to heart with the divine

EVERY DAY GOD

david hose and *takeko hose*

wisdom tree

First published by Beyond Words Publishing, Inc., Hillsboro, Oregon

ISBN 81-86685-42-1

Published in 2003 by
Wisdom Tree
C-209/1, Mayapuri II,
New Delhi 110 064
Ph.: 28111720, 28114437

Printed at
Print Perfect
New Delhi 110 064

Each moment contains a hundred messages from God:

To every cry of "Oh, Lord,"

He answers a hundred times, "I am here."

—RUMI

CONTENTS

PROLOGUE

SOMETIMES we are blessed with grace, and in a quiet moment we unexpectedly move beyond our everyday struggles and touch a place of inner peace. At such moments we are reminded that we are not alone, that there's a greater power which is a part of our lives. Sometimes, however, this same grace comes at seemingly unbearable personal expense. In our case, it was the latter. But if there is one thing we've learned, it is that the cost of confirming our relationship with God, or a higher power, can never diminish what we have gained.

For me, the story begins in a hotel room in California; for my wife, Takeko, it begins in her beloved garden in New York. Just two weeks before, in mid-October, I'd secured a lucrative Christmas job in Los Angeles, leaving my family back home in Tarrytown. Having completed my first day of management training, I decided to reward myself with a night at a good hotel. I planned to spend some time meditating about the near future and then to get a good night's sleep. Right after dinner, I went to my room with plans to call Takeko. But first I called my sister in nearby Woodland Hills to let her know how the day had gone and when she could expect a visit from me. I no sooner said hello than she blurted out, "David, there's been a very serious accident. It's Takeko. She was accidentally shot by your son. Call home right away."

Badly shaken, I immediately dialed my home number. A family friend answered and related what had happened. Takeko had been pruning an apple tree in the shadowy garden area behind our home. Our oldest son thought she was a garden-raiding deer and fired two shots to scare it away from his mother's precious orchard. Crumpling to the ground on suddenly lifeless legs, Takeko cried out for our son, hoping he'd come from the house. Instead, he emerged, rifle in hand, from the nearby brush. In the next horrible moments, mother and son realized what had happened. Takeko prayed for survival while our son raced her off to the emergency room.

My son had purchased the .22 rifle the previous summer. We'd been against it, but he pleaded and assured us that he'd use it only for target practice. In the face of his expert persuasion, we had relented. After a few weeks, the threat of having a gun in our house faded. Besides, we were preoccupied with planning an upcoming move to Seattle and how we would announce the move to our children.

Even as my friend was telling me that the doctors were not sure that Takeko was going to make it, our son was being interrogated by several policemen in our living room. One of the younger officers, my friend told me, was quite convinced the shooting was premeditated.

The next hours were a blur as I booked a red-eye special back home. After an interminable flight, not knowing if I'd ever see my wife alive again, I deplaned in a crowded terminal and was driven immediately to the hospital where Takeko was in intensive care. In the waiting room I was greeted by familiar faces—friends who were not quite certain of what to say or do. After tearful hugs, a nurse came out and ushered me into Takeko's room. Surrounded by IV poles, monitoring equipment, and a stoic-looking medical staff, my dear wife looked pale and small. Tubes protruded from her mouth and side. She smiled at me as I leaned over her bed, as if to assure me that she would make it.

After five hours of emergency surgery, I was told, the team of doctors had upgraded her chance of survival. I sighed with relief. Hell brightened and I thanked God.

I stayed at Takeko's side for only a few moments and then reluctantly whispered good-bye. The neurologist followed me into the hallway and described the injuries. One bullet had smashed into Takeko's spinal area, damaging nerves to her legs. She would probably never walk again. As bad as this news was, it was enough to know that she was going to live.

As I returned to the waiting room, my son came rushing up to me. He sobbed into my shoulder, trying to explain what had happened. It wasn't a time for fatherly chastening. I just held him. Whatever agony I'd experienced on the long plane ride from Los Angeles couldn't begin to compare with the agony of what he was going through.

After a few moments the two of us went back to Takeko's room. She smiled as we went to her side, and then she scrawled a note to our son on a pad of paper the nurse supplied. "Why aren't you in school?" it said. He gazed at her in shock. She wrote again, "Don't worry. I'm going to make it. You better go back to school."

Our son later told us that those notes gave him more encouragement than anything else during those first days following the accident. After Takeko regained her speech, she quietly told our son that she felt no blame or anger toward him. He had made a mistake, but he mustn't allow himself to be destroyed by guilt. Today Takeko is convinced that the shooting opened a door in her relationship with our son. It deepened their relationship in a way that seemed almost miraculous.

In late November, Takeko was transferred to a rehabilitation hospital. Her new home was the spinal cord injury and amputee ward. Here she would undergo an intensive physical and occupational therapy program to help her adapt to the realities of a wheelchair lifestyle and constant pain.

With the coming of the new year, I set about preparing the house for Takeko's return. I installed a ramp to our main-floor hallway and cleared passageways throughout the house so that her wheelchair could move about easily. In February, we drove from the rehabilitation center through a sunny but frigid Hudson Valley, arriving home late in the morning. After a jerky wheelchair ride from the back porch to our bedroom, Takeko at last lay on our large double bed. She'd lost twenty pounds since the accident in October, most of it in muscle mass from her legs. The strong legs that had carried our family for so many years were now shrunken to the circumference of a small child's.

Nonstop spasms contorted her upper legs, and she uttered little cries as they rippled through the muscles. I sat next to her, trying to somehow comfort her. The giant blue diaper she had to wear for lack of bowel control heaped mocking insult on an already devastating injury.

One by one the kids arrived and embraced their mother. In spite of everything, it was so good to have her back home. The heart of our family had returned.

We'd decided earlier in the day that we would pray each night after everyone else had gone to bed. Someone who had once experienced their own dark night of the soul said that the essence of prayer is a cry for help. Never was that more true than for Takeko and me that night in early February. There was little else we could do. I sat next to her on the bed, and we began to pray.

We both wanted this communication badly—like an instinctual hunger. For Takeko, there was nothing philosophical involved. Would her pain ever end? Would she ever walk again? What about our previous plans to move to the West Coast? Would all this have to change? And what about our finances?

I had not yet shared my own concerns with Takeko. There was a painful issue that my time alone with the children had unearthed: I didn't really know them! For too many years in my work with the church, I'd been running around the world trying to help other people's children. God's will, for me, had been the next set of directives and plane tickets from my department head. God had become my commander, always ready with another battle plan. But now I was having to face the fact that by being gone over forty weeks per year for a decade, I had robbed my own children of their father. I now sought guidance from a higher power on how I would heal all this.

In the months since the accident, God had been MIA for me. My relationship with God felt about as unresolved as my relationship with my kids. Deep down, I confess, I didn't really like Him. No wonder! I'd created Him in my own image. Suddenly, after twenty years of working for God, I was asking, "Who is this God?"

From that first night of Takeko's return, our prayers were unlike any I had ever experienced. I'd been praying in groups throughout my life, though I had never relished it, even in the years since I had developed a public eloquence. Prayer, for me, had been from the neck up. Always my voice had echoed back to me. I'd wondered, "Am I heard? Do I really mean this?"

The first nights that Takeko and I prayed together, we wept. In the presence of my wife's agony, it would have been impossible for even the coldest of souls to pray neck-up prayers. My own tears were also tears of peace, of knowing that I was returning from a long distance to a God that I now understand I had never allowed myself to know. And so the tears flowed from both of us.

Many questions arose those first nights. What do we pray for? Do we pray for healing? I remembered watching evangelists on television in the 1950s, seeing crutches thrown aside and wheelchairs abandoned. And certainly, those first nights of prayer together did find us asking for Takeko's legs back and for an end to her pain.

But something more was emerging, something quite unexpected. In the life of Christ, it seems clear that healing the lame was not his most essential work. Far greater was the inward healing of the heart. I remembered his last words: "Father, forgive them, for they know not what they do." This statement of love in the face of such hatred surely mirrors the plight of humanity—of killing one another even as we hold the knowledge of our oneness.

This profound lesson echoed in our own lives. These prayers were not just about Takeko's legs or her pain. Our prayers were about our son, who had certainly not intended this to happen to our family. And they were about me, about my absence from the family for so many years and how it had affected those I love.

As our prayers continued, a theme emerged. We soon found ourselves putting the whole of our situation into God's hands, for whatever purpose He deemed good. Takeko and I confirmed in our hearts and minds that beyond her daily struggle with pain, we wished to dedicate our lives in the service of God.

A couple weeks into these prayer sessions, I began noticing a warm sensation around my heart. It felt as if my heart were filling—I know this is a strange image—with *helium gas*! It felt pleasantly light and full. Even more than this was a feeling of the deepest love for my wife. Another love, far beyond our own, was embracing the two of us together. I didn't mention this to Takeko at first. Several years before, I'd had a mediumistic experience connected with a particularly traumatic event. It seemed to me that talking about what I was now feeling would trigger memories that I did not want to open up again.

While I felt cautious, I could not deny that this love, and the desire to tell Takeko about it, kept building. As she began her prayers one evening, I asked her to stop, to wait. As she turned to listen, I said, "All I can say is that there is this feeling of incredible love for you. It's been building night by night, and it isn't just me. I mean, I do love you a lot, but this is something much more."

I described the loving presence that communicated wordlessly during our prayers. I wanted to share the message with which this presence encompassed us. I told her I would keep the messages of this being in the third person as I related what I was experiencing. Takeko was calm and ready to listen.

I closed my eyes and began. Whatever original intentions I had to speak in the third person were swept away like a feather by an ocean wave. As my tears flowed, I immediately knew they were of a different quality than those I'd shed that first night. These tears flowed from a far deeper place within my heart. The voice that came pouring forth was in the first person, with such love and depth that I could barely convey it. I was as moved by the words that were being expressed through my own mouth as was my quietly weeping partner. I felt sorely at a loss to translate into a suddenly limited earthly language the love pouring out through my heart. And I could not curb the flow of tears that washed down my face as I experienced this loving presence.

That first communication lasted for over an hour, during which time Takeko and I felt enveloped in a loving embrace beyond anything we'd ever experienced. When it finally stopped and Takeko was "tucked in for the night," I lay filled with amazement and gratitude. But I couldn't imagine that it would ever be repeated. I was wrong. This was just the opening!

The following night, the same warmth and overwhelming love returned.

Again the expressions flowed through my own heart and voice, taking up from where it had left off the previous night. A third and fourth night passed the same way. I knew this wasn't mediumship or channeling. It was not a spirit speaking through me. It was God speaking from within yet beyond within. Regrettably, we didn't think to record the expressions of those first several nights, but their message remains in our hearts.

The love that embraced us was that of a parent. At one point He compared Takeko's injury to His own, saying that He, too, was impaired at the place where He touched the Earth. He spoke of the spiritual unconsciousness of humanity that was much like the numbness and pain of Takeko's legs.

From the beginning He was natural and totally spontaneous. He told us He has always been with us, as with each and every person. But so many of us have become estranged, cut off from that part of us where we encounter Him face-to-face. He spoke of moments when each person, through whatever circumstances, comes to this place within himself and experiences this encounter. Too often we overlook these encounters with God, consigning them to memory, attributing them to our own inventiveness, or simply forgetting in the ocean of everyday experiences. The message conveyed was that this encounter—this relationship with our Selves and with Him—should be the easiest and most natural thing in our lives. We were often told, "I am not going away after a few nights with you. I am here always."

If our moment of encounter was triggered by Takeko's desperate situation, our urgent and innocent prayers had brought us to that place within our hearts where this contact is made. We were told that though we might pull away, He would always be waiting, as He has always done, for every heart.

He told us not to think of religion as being the only way to Him. Rather, the place of true communion with Him is within each person's heart. The original beauty and magnificence of the human heart, He taught us, is far greater than the greatest cathedrals and still remains the place where He communicates best with us. With humor, He confided that He was "never really the religious type"! Tearfully, He confided that He was really the family type, meaning the family of all humanity. Sadly, He reflected, only a few of His sons and daughters allow themselves to feel this original connection with Him, much less with each other. Most do not even believe it possible.

Soon, we began to tape these sessions. Takeko and I were always together for them, and so it remains to this day. While the expressions came through my voice, it is clear that Takeko's quiet faith and love of God provided the space in our lives for this opening to occur.

Soon after we started recording the sessions, we decided to share them with a few close friends. We circulated typewritten transcriptions, and this soon became a large network that has now spread around the world. And then, people urged us to put these readings together in a book. But before that could happen, Takeko and I had much work to do in our own lives.

One's life is not instantly changed or perfected as a result of experiences like those we share in this book. God is clearly not a spiritual surgeon who reshapes our inner selves with a few well-placed divine pronouncements. The process of learning to look at ourselves through the clearer lens of the inner eye (the "inner I") and grow beyond our fears, skepticism, blaming, and all the rest of our immaturities is lovingly placed in our own hands.

Before reading on, let me warn you: This is not a book about one woman's miraculous recovery from gunshot wounds, paralysis, and pain, though God has certainly helped us understand Takeko's injuries and has brought much spiritual comfort. Rather, He speaks through us of healing a more fundamental injury, an injury within the heart due to humanity's fracturing of the circle of Divine Love.

As you read the pages to come, it should be noted that in "translating" the language of the heart, the person who receives and articulates this information—in this case, me—is in the process of his own personal growth and change. This will color both how I receive these messages and how I am able to express them.

Also, as you read, remember that each of us has our own perceptual filters, or unique library of experiences, and these will color how you perceive what I share with you. Though I have done my very best, from moment to moment, to convey His messages accurately, you may find yourself having to look beyond the veils of my language and experience and thus into your own heart to discover the truth that you will find there. You are the final and most important translator.

These writings can never replace your own direct experiences of God, the face-to-face encounter you can have with Him. But we sincerely hope that this book will serve as inspiration and confirmation for your own unique path of opening your heart to a more direct communion with God.

ACKNOWLEDGMENTS

OUR first and deepest gratitude goes to God, who has been here with us long before either the conception of this book or the experiences that inspired it.

During the early '90s, when we simply wanted to share these talks with our friends, Joyce James and Leslie Ebata helped with transcribing and editing the tape recordings we'd made. Their belief, unconditional efforts, and countless hours of work helped to give us a sure vision for continuing this work. Our thanks to both of them.

Three dear people patiently listened to our plans, volunteered their help, and worked with us as a team: Sally Cole, Sylvia Norton, and Barbara Ten Wolde. Their energy and spirit carried us even when our own energy was lagging. Our deepest thanks to them for their strength, sensitivity, and tenacity in making certain that this book came together.

Early in our efforts to contact a publishing company for our project, our friend Steve Evans called us. He had struck up a conversation with Richard Cohn, a publisher, in the checkout line at the grocery store. Thanks to Steve's serendipitous meeting, we connected with Richard Cohn and Cindy Black, co-founders of Beyond Words Publishing, Inc. Our many thanks to them both for their support of *Every Day God* and for the growing vision that guides their wonderful publishing house.

Hal Zina Bennett, our editor, himself the author of thirty published books, has handled the text with sensitivity, thoughtfulness, and beautiful restraint. Any apprehensions we had about how an editor would handle this material were laid to rest. And the astute eye of Marvin Moore, our proofreader, found errors the rest of us missed. Many thanks to them both.

Finally, we would like to thank some special souls who have helped us in various important ways over the past several years: Stephen Pfaender has given tremendous help with communications. His friendship, input, and willingness to help us clarify our vision have been invaluable. Mrs. Mee Shik Choi has been of great support at critical junctures in our lives. Our gratitude also goes out to Jeff and Miyako Gledhill, Sigi and Christine Pracher, Tim Folzenlogen, Hans Tolzin, Jonathan Slevin, Carol Bechtel, John Biermans, Michael Breen, Ron and Connie Pappalardo, and so many others whose assistance has kept us going.

Last and certainly not least, we would like to thank our children, who've supported us through everything.

David and Takeko have initiated a Web site to keep readers updated on their activities and to provide a forum for like-minded individuals:

WWW.EVERYDAYGOD.NET

AN INTRODUCTION FROM GOD

THANK YOU for taking the time to open this book. As you read about this couple's experiences you will probably have one of a variety of reactions, according to your own experiences: Many of you will already have had communications similar to what David and Takeko report here, and what you read here will be not a surprise for you but rather a confirmation. Or perhaps you have never had such an experience, in which case you may find yourself wondering how David and Takeko could even claim to have this kind of communion with the Almighty. Indeed, this book may challenge your understanding of how the world works.

Whatever your experience, know that the messages in this book come from One who loves you most deeply. This book speaks to something that each and every one of you possesses—the potential to have full and unhindered communication between you and Me. This form of communication reaches far beyond any you have ever known in your daily, outward experience. Often, it does not involve words as you know them but comes from deep within your heart. It is an intimate communication that you will realize you have known from the day of your birth.

David Hose, My translator for these messages, calls it the language of the heart. Though there are those who might like to discuss this process, it is not necessary for Me to do so. What is covered here is not theoretical, nor has it ever been a matter to be argued back and forth. Nor is it important for this communication to be perfect. There never has been a perfect and complete expression of what I desire to communicate to you. This sharing will never be captured by paper and ink. Rather, this sharing is a living communion that lives in your innermost heart and that is eternally evolving.

Throughout the millennia I have longed for full, deep, intimate communion with each of you; it is a very large part of why you were created. Yet the history of those spiritual seekers who have found this place of genuine communion with Me has often been sad and even tragic. I have seen innocent and open hearts denied and even condemned by those who judged them as heretics or as abnormal and dangerous. Beautiful sons and daughters have been imprisoned, driven out, tortured, and even killed by those who could not or would not understand. Then—often a decade, a century, a millennium after the persecution—those same martyred innocents were praised or sainted or in some cases even given the status of deities.

Please understand in your heart that neither the persecution nor the worship were right. Both those who persecuted and those who worshiped, almost without exception, failed to consider the sacred within themselves; instead, they saw those they sainted or deified as having special abilities. They missed the point that each and every one of you has the same abilities, the same capacities to have this deep communion with Me. Longing to be known by each of you, I worked through those innocent souls, incomplete though our communications may have been.

What is important to Me, far beyond this book, is your knowing that you have an inherent capacity for communicating directly and fully with Me. This book and any other expressions coming from outside your own wondrous heart are but dim testimonies to the potential that you have. This realization—the acceptance of what is within you—is central to the future of humanity.

How do you communicate with Me? How does it work to communicate within the heart? Whether in sending or receiving, the human heart is the finest communication system in all of Creation! Do you ever picture God as living in an idyllic place somewhere within or outside of Creation? Please understand that there could never be a better place for My presence than within your own heart as I created it. Beyond the flesh-and-blood organ that supports your physical life, your spiritual heart is the jewel of jewels. I could want for no greater palace. If you, in this moment, could fully observe the beauty, the awesomeness of what is at your very core, you would dissolve into a sea of tears.

How can you know this heart within you? Your knowing begins with an awareness of what David calls "the impulse of the heart," so let us call it that. This impulse of your heart is not referring to the daily emotions you know so well, stimulated by objects or people around you—sexual feelings, hunger or thirst for food or drink, the desire for entertainment or possessions, and so on. The impulse of the heart that I speak of here arises from within the heart itself.

The impulse of your heart involves an inner reality that only a few have come to understand. These few are not of a "chosen" or elite group. They are no different from you. It is simply that at some point in their lives, whether from an early age or through life's challenges—yes, sometimes extreme circumstances—they had a growing awareness of this impulse and responded to its call. What they and I would tell you, with the deepest love, is that this impulse is within each of you, without exception. It is your inheritance as a child of God.

Human history is full of those who did not, for whatever reasons, heed this impulse, this voice from within. At many times in your life you may have suspected My presence in that very voice. Yes, it was Me. And you so often chose not to listen. Perhaps you made this decision out of fear or out of a belief that what you were hearing or feeling was not real. Or perhaps you dismissed what you heard or rejected it because you did not want others to think of you as abnormal or strange. Or you may have felt that I could not possibly be communicating with you because you believed you were not worthy. There have perhaps been as many reasons for not hearing Me as there are people in all of history.

For a moment, let Me speak to you who hold as a tenet of your faith that you are sinners. For each of you, preceding any sinful act is the fundamental sin of separation between us. Regardless of how you may have learned to live a disciplined and consistent life within the moral teachings of your faith, this fundamental sin of separation will not be resolved until you open your heart to daily communication with Me. I know that this is a complicated and thorny issue, but please understand My perspective: You are, first and before anything, My son, My daughter. I don't look at you from the outside in; I look from the inside out. At the very innermost core of yourself, at the very heart of your being, is the place where we meet completely and perfectly, where no separation can or ever would exist. It is the root of your being as a daughter, a son of Divine Parentage.

Don't dignify what you so often have called your fallen nature by giving it equal status with the true nature of who you are as a son or daughter. At the end of the day, when you see your own child covered with grime from play, you want to put that child in the tub and clean him up. The significance of that dirt on your child doesn't begin to compare with the beauty which lies beneath it—the child's essence and the love you feel in her or his presence. And that is how I look at what you have called your sins. What you may see as your shortcomings or transgressions are as so much dust compared to the spiritual essence that we share in your innermost heart.

I want to help you remove the dust from your long journey. The tragic thing for both of us is that you feel you cannot come to Me until you are perfectly clean. You think of Me as someone so high and holy, so truly untouchable, that I become a fearful Being in your sight. This idea, taught by many of your religious institutions, by leaders and followers alike, has succeeded in driving so many away from even the thought of enjoying a genuine relationship with Me.

Most religious institutions were, at their foundations, inspired by an impulse of the heart, but that impulse has so often become buried under altars of stone. *I am your parent!* If you, in your deepest heart, honor the absolute honesty and intimacy that can dwell between parent and child, then know that this thought, this impulse for such a relationship, comes from Me. I honor it and long for that communion with you. You are worthy of our love together. But I cannot get My love through to you if you are convinced that you are not worthy of receiving it.

Think of a child caught up in the idea that he is unworthy of his parents' love. What if the child feels that his parents would reject him because he soiled his clothes or didn't live up to their expectations of him? This dark concept would block the flow of love between child and parent. The parents could not force love on the child, for it takes two to create such a bond. Overruled by the child's concept of unworthiness, the parent would be prevented from letting the child know of his or her love. The child cannot hear the voice of his or her love—not because that love isn't there but because the child's sense of unworthiness has blocked him from receiving it.

It is the same in your relationship with Me. When you feel unworthy, I am as confined by your feelings of unworthiness as you are. Is the child who clings to the concept of unworthiness any different from children thinking themselves too good for their parents and thus not in need of them? Be it too good or not good enough, the effect is the same. It hinders the powerful embrace that can finally erase what you may have perceived as sin and what I call separation.

At some point in your life, or perhaps at many, you may have experienced an impulse of your heart. However fleeting it might have been, it is totally different from the many mundane moments of daily life. Most likely you didn't forget this special moment, and even today you may be curious about it. You may have wondered about its source or longed for it to happen again.

David used to give sermons on a regular basis. During the course of his presentations he often experienced insights that seemed to bubble up out of nowhere. They were wonderful insights, and they moved him and his audiences. He would think that they must come from him—his creativity at work—and that he was just gifted that way. In the ensuing years I have told him that he was not creating or realizing them on his own. At those moments we were working together, and often in our relationship these promptings came from Me. Still, it took David several years and much work to fully accept My part in these messages. I mention this example because you often dismiss too easily these moments that could turn into a real journey together with Me.

Three hundred years before Jesus' birth, Mencius, a great Chinese philosopher and spiritual teacher, advised, "The great man is he who does not lose his child's-heart." Jesus and other spiritual teachers have spoken much of regaining this child's-heart, since it is with the innocence of this heart that you will open to Me. This is a simple but deeply profound invitation. The impulse of the heart is a signal for you, beckoning you toward childlike openness where the "sin" of separation from Me is dissolved forever.

This book is the story of one couple who, in the midst of extreme circumstances in their own lives, opened to My voice from within their own hearts. From their experience a huge amount of material was translated from this language of the heart into the words you read in these pages. By no means is it a perfect translation. In fact, even as we communicated, David was many times bothered by self-doubt: "Is this really happening? Is it just my invention? What happens if I ask for this communion and nothing comes? I'm too tired tonight. Let's just go to sleep." Even now he's learning to embrace greater simplicity in all of this.

Please look beyond the translation that David has provided. Look into your own heart and life experience for confirmation. Ask yourself what you truly want and who will bring it to you. Once you have opened to your own inner heart, other opportunities will come to you to communicate directly and wholly with Me.

There will be more and more books like this in the future, written by many translators; the messages will be wrapped in different personalities and backgrounds, each of them unique. But please look inside the wrappings, for the books are not the final point. The final point lies within the magnificence of your own heart.

1

Being Your Honest Self with Me

The key to a truly honest relationship with Me is found in your own heart. Here you will also find the key to your life, to your empowerment, to your freedom, to your effectiveness, and to your self-understanding.

BECAUSE your prayers are so important to Me, it is vital to discuss how this communication can shape the kind of relationship you will have with Me.

I must tell you honestly that I don't like what the word *prayer* has come to mean for so many of My children. What is called prayer is often little more than ritualized expression. Sometimes it is even written in books and read to Me or memorized. How would you like it if your friends communicated with you only by reading from books? I'm sure you wouldn't call that real communication. Well, I am your friend. I am your closest friend and your parent. I don't find much pleasure in such communication either. People should not think that they must limit what they say to Me or confine themselves to particular concepts about how these communications should occur.

Many people pray for great things—for the world to be changed, for goodness to come to a people or a continent, and so on. But if that prayer is offered only as a kind of duty or obligation and doesn't truly come from their own heart, then it doesn't touch My heart and it doesn't touch the hearts of those in the realm of spirit who hear it. What touches My heart is your heartfelt expression, that which comes from your being.

When you go to a person whose friendship you treasure, do you not open up to them? Is that not truly a time when you can feel closest to your dear friend, whether you are talking about yourself, your deepest secrets, or your concerns for this or that person or situation and all that you dream of? You come away from such moments together feeling almost as if you've taken a spiritual shower.

That friend may strongly disagree with you or think you are hurting yourself by thinking the thoughts you have expressed. You may agree or disagree with what he or she tells you. But whatever your friend says—when that person's expressions come from their deepest love for you—you feel a sense of true appreciation, knowing that you are loved with the greatest love your friend could offer. And that friend, too, feels the treasure of your friendship, of your trust that you express with this person the things you cannot easily share with anyone else in the world.

Think of Me always in this same way—as that kind of friend. As a friend, I don't want you to have limiting concepts about how to communicate with Me or what you can or cannot share with Me through prayer. If it helps you, do not use the word *prayer* to describe these moments with Me. Speak instead of *talking* with Me, *sharing* with Me.

All the earthly doctrines about what prayer is or isn't keep you up in your head. They keep you from going down into your heart to truly mine the treasures that are there. Your head is a storage place for memories and reactions—patterns of life that come to you from the past. It is not the place from which to reach Me. Your heart is the living place within you where your whole being comes into direct communication with Me.

When you come deeply from your heart, I hear all that you say, and every word from your heart goes deeply into My heart. That is what communication between us means. You may worry that if you really share everything that is in your heart it may sound childish or self-centered or you may end up crying and bearing ignoble realities about your own life. But that is where we begin! That is where relationship is made.

As you sit with a friend over lunch, would you feel that you must converse only in a certain, set way and only about noble realities and ideals but without really communicating, or would you rather feel that you can be open, honest, and frank with one another, truly expressing your beings, even if the things you speak of are not high and noble?

Well, I am no different. I know you worry about what might come out or how you might say it. But we have to start somewhere. And if that honesty and truth of your being involves pain or involves expressing things that have nothing to do with saving the world, if it just has to do with calling for help for yourself, I want you to know that I am here! I am here, and I know this is where we begin—with your truest heartfelt expressions.

You see, I trust that as you express your pain and as you go through those many different levels of your being, what is in your deepest heart has everything to do with the establishment of a true and good world. Even when this is the very subject you want to discuss with Me, you need not express yourself through heady platitudes about saving this or that country or helping people who are suffering great hardships. Nor do you have to remember this or that saint in your communications with Me.

I'm tired of slogans! I want to go to the real depths with you, because one prayer expressed from those depths—even one short sentence in behalf of you or another, or in behalf of a country, a people, or whatever—means far more to Me than hours and hours of prayers from the head, however high the ideals that you might be trying to express. One word from your heart means so much more to Me than volumes of words from your head.

Your world is awash in words that are severed from the heart. You may say only what you think others want to hear, especially when you look up to those in authority—tragically, even when you look to Me as an authority that you must please. If you look closely at your world you will understand that there is no power in this. Sadly, it only breeds spiritual dishonesty. Many people's whole identities are based on untruths such as these expressions that come from being disconnected from what is in their own hearts.

It is time to see Me in a new light, to see Me as I am. And I long to see you as you are.

We've talked about these things before, but I shall come back to these themes every once in a while just to reemphasize their importance. You can agree with what I may have told you about these things last month or last year. But with each new experience of your life you may see it in a new light and express yourself in a more heartfelt way to Me. Then I say, "Yes! Yes, I know. Open up to Me! Let Me know your heart!" And when you do, we really make progress together.

I want so much to be fully expressed in each one of your lives. Let your relationship with Me, through prayer, become your foundation. When you can truly communicate with Me and I can truly communicate with you, then more and more we will become—in every sense—at one in our direction.

This does not happen instantaneously. Your communications with Me will not be perfected in a day or a week. Our relationship will build in a cumulative way. As time goes by you will find your life full of magnificent power—the power of truthfulness, the power of expressing who you truly are in the deepest sense—the power that comes from having no fear, no shame!

Fear and shame are great cripplers. They come from dishonesty, and they also cause dishonesty. They cause you to hold back who you truly are—in your relationship with Me and consequently in your relationships with one another. Fear, shame, and dishonesty cause a split in your personality. When you know you are accepted in full, without any hesitation, without any limits placed on your own communication, this becomes the basis for a whole different way of life. It will transform your daily dealings with the world.

I am grateful for these moments when you are honest, even when they involve struggling with your own situation. I am grateful for these times. But for you to be honest with Me doesn't have to rise only out of such desperate, dark moments. You can learn to maintain honest communication with Me always.

Please observe yourself, and know that you have the capacity and absolute freedom to be fully honest with Me and true in our communication, whether in times of great desperation and difficulty or in times when things are going well for you. Keep up these moments of heartfelt communication with Me through difficult times but also through those times when you are more relaxed, when you are able to take your daily life for granted and be at ease.

I need direct, honest communication as much as you do. I want it even more than you do. It liberates Me to fully and freely attend to both your immediate needs and the needs of the entire world around you.

This kind of communication is possible for each and every person. Each and every one of you must learn that the key to a truly honest relationship with Me is found in your own heart. And in this heartfelt honesty you will also find the key to your life, to your empowerment, to your freedom, to your effectiveness, and to your self-understanding.

I recognize how you care for and love the world and want human suffering to stop. These feelings are present in your deepest heart. You don't have to form the words in your mind or follow the dictates of any particular doctrine to discover how to pray for your human family. Your deepest connection with your human family is in your heart and in the honest relationship you have with Me. It will come as automatically and as freely as water flows down the side of a mountain. And it won't stop. It will wash out the valleys of pain and suffering around you because it comes right out of My heart. Our hearts share a single root.

I know that there are times when you are faced with great difficulties in your lives, difficulties that are very personal, difficulties having to do with your concern about loved ones, family members, one of your own children if you are a parent, or yourself. And many of you believe that you cannot come to Me with such problems, perhaps because they are selfish needs. Many of you have been taught that you should not bother this "Mighty God on High" but should carefully compose what you wish to pray. Some ways of thought teach this, and it becomes a habit for you. But remind yourself always that the key to your relationship with Me is found here in the words I have shared with you today, that communicating from your most honest inner being is what is important to Me.

I love you very deeply.

2

Awakening from the Long Sleep

Humanity has been in a profound sleep. It is the sleep of projecting your own realities—the dreams that you have created out of your unconsciousness of Me.

YOU have been exploring the meaning of maturity and learning that it is not gained through intellectual efforts or college degrees. Rather, it comes by opening your heart and communicating directly with Me, being fully aware of My perspective on the world. When I say *perspective*, it's not just a personal viewpoint about the world—it is a consciousness of the world. But words are limiting and do not express My full intention on this point.

Your world is in My heart, and I have completely absorbed that world, from so long ago, even before it was created. In that way, you see that I do not simply mean an intellectual perspective or a certain opinion; it is an awareness of what that world truly is.

What could I do after what you call the human Fall? It was very painful because that world which was so deeply and fully a part of My heart had exploded with an outbreak of evil, a separation from My original ideal. What could I do? Even after the explosion, good or not good, that world is still in My heart.

My one concern has been to restore that world to its rightful place. As you share more, and as your life becomes more and more open, surely you feel a hunger—a desire for the original ideal. When you see inner blindness, shortsightedness, narrowness, and all of those human emotions that don't fit the original perspective, it becomes painful. As you awaken, not only do you see these in other people, but you have to see them in yourself. That's a very natural thing. It's not something you need to be taught.

I know that each time you awaken from those moments of having slipped back into the deep sleep of separation from Me, you say, "Oh, no, I did it again!" No one has to tell you. It's not a matter of defending yourself in the eyes of other people or desperately searching for and proclaiming your dignity as people sometimes do. It's simply a matter of beginning to see in a whole new way. You no longer feel the desperate drive to be recognized or lifted up in any way that is not of Me. You simply want to become more and more alive, more and more awake in this very different but ageless knowledge.

And I do see you awakening. Don't you know I'm right here to shake you, to kiss your cheek, to encourage you, to open up the draperies and show you the bright morning sun? Sometimes a child wants to roll away from the light, pull the blanket over his head, and go back into that sleep. But I cannot let you, because I know what is waiting for you as you swing your feet out and put them on the floor, becoming grounded in that true awakening which is coming.

I want to do this with each of you. Humanity has been in a profound sleep. It is the sleep of projecting your own realities—the dreams that you have created out of your unconsciousness of Me. You even project your own image of what I am like!

Some see Me as an angry, vengeful God who wants to destroy all that is evil. Some see Me as a forgiving God who wants to release His enemies. Some see Me as an uncaring God who believes the human race is already lost and has moved on to other matters in other parts of the universe. And you live according to how you see Me. Many have no thought of Me at all; I'm not a part of their conscious reality.

Many religious people don't want to hear this, of course, especially if they have studied their Scriptures and followed great holy men and women who have become their role models. They try to live righteous lives. Still, in so many cases even those religious ones project their personal pictures of Me onto the world. They generate their own gods, and sometimes they fight among themselves, arguing who is right and who is wrong and which of them God loves the most.

And you, in this moment, could easily do that also. You get a certain message, you have a certain experience, and then something in you says, "Now I know! I know and you don't know. Therefore, you need to know what I know." So with whatever knowledge you've understood—who God is, what God's will is—you go marching into the world confident that you know something which others don't.

You will never achieve anything of lasting value as long as you hold this attitude. The risk of greater separation from Me becomes larger and larger. Here is the problem of so many righteous people: They become self-righteous. The self becomes too big. When this happens, it is no longer the true self; it's a concept. The ego has taken over.

Takeko and David, I speak to you now, using your example as a lesson for others. What if you and I had had just one meaningful communication four years ago? What if you had spent the next four years just testifying to how great that was and how much you learned through it? Wouldn't there have been some part of you saying, "Is that the only communication we'll ever have?"

Your testimony may be good, but is there not another part of you that would ask, "Shouldn't there be more than just this one communication? Shouldn't it go on moment by moment?" And you would be right. The truth is not just in that single, wonderful communication we had four years ago. The truth, ultimately, is in our moment-by-moment relationship.

Now, this is a very delicate matter. A lot of problems are created when you are not fully mature yet think you have a profound relationship with Me. You then go marching out into the world with your message. I am sure that if you examine the state of our relationship at this moment you may find yourself rolling away and pulling a blanket over your head many times during the day—getting lost in anger or hurt and feeling emotions that have nothing to do with Me. So, along with the conviction that you want to share everything about God, you go out into the world with these emotions which are yours and yours alone.

It's a long journey to come to the point of full maturity, to the state where you and I can work together consciously without those lapses into spiritual sleep day after day. It's a kind of spiritual growing up. But it is a journey that must be made if your life is to be completely fulfilled and if the world around you is to be enlightened by what is in your own heart. And so it is with each and every person, not just you, David and Takeko.

Throughout history people have received My message not through their own spiritual experiences but through another person's spiritual enlightenment. They receive that insight and might in fact have a profound conversion, but then they go out into the world proclaiming, "Now I know. Now I will change the world according to what I see."

Through the centuries this has been helpful, because without any knowledge of Me the world would quickly sink to even far greater depths of darkness. So any forward step that religion has fostered is good. The steps that have already been made have brought humanity to a certain level. But by the very nature and circumstances of the world today, we see that many more steps are needed. And the very steps that are needed are the steps of the individual awakening to Me. This day-by-day, moment-by-moment relationship with Me is the Truth you seek.

All of the religious book-learning in the world—even the memorization of the entire Bible, which I know some people have done—doesn't mean a thing if those words are just locked up in your head. You may be able to quote any verse at any moment—which in itself is an extraordinary accomplishment—but is that true knowledge? No, it is not.

There are men and women who were locked away in prison for years by unspeakably evil authorities. They had no holy books to guide them, but they quietly made that bond with Me. I know them; they are for Me very special beings. The only thing that kept them sane, the only thing that kept them alive, was their secret connection with Me. They had nothing by earthly standards, yet their hearts reached out for Me. And in the bond that we formed something special came to be.

When people are subjected to unusual pressures, when they suffer great hardships or pain, they often come to recognize that what once gave them confidence is no longer enough. It is no different for you. It does not matter if your source of strength was religion or perhaps a prestigious position you once held in your life. Suddenly, you recognize that you need something more to sustain you.

It is very painful for Me to watch your people choosing paths that carry them further and further from that state of being awake. Too many just want to sleep in a deep, soft bed, full of dreams, full of illusions, experiencing more and more separation and even evil.

Sooner or later your nation will need a tremendous jolt to awaken it. Not all people are unrighteous, of course, but the strain now growing like cancer in a body is alarming even to Me. When you get further and further away from that waking state, you sink more and more into your dreams, where anything can happen. There's no foundation, no substance in that sleep; there's no guidance system. That's why this awakening is so necessary.

This awakening is unique. It is very different from anything you have seen on this planet before. The entire history of your planet is now focusing on this new awakening—the awakening of each individual. If the atom is seen as the basic unit upon which the life of your body is based, and if each atom is corrupted and isn't functioning correctly, your body is immediately gone. In this same way, each individual is a basic unit of reality.

The whole world could be gradually lifted up by certain religious revelations, but finally it must happen within each heart and not just from outside campaigns. It's not a matter of motivation by the media or a minister or spiritual leader. Each heart has to awaken to Me, to the very quiet voice within.

Historically, there would be one form of semi-awakening, and then the next semi-awakening would come from a different direction. The earlier force might then fight the next and try to suppress it, causing massive conflicts. Each singular force of enlightenment becomes so confident that they are The Answer that when the next level of answers are offered they do not hear them but only become defensive. You see that in your own experience. When you and I began this communication—and as I begin it with each and every person—those who previously offered you answers became a source of conflict. They do not want you to move on or to move away from them.

Each of you must become conscious of self-righteousness, of thinking of yourself as having the answer. Each of you must reflect on yourself as you see those around you becoming defensive in their confidence that they know the way. Don't be angry toward anything or anyone outside of you. Instead, rededicate yourself to your truth. Rededicate yourself to waking up.

And pray. Stay close with Me in praying for the day that this awakening will spread far and wide. And do all you can to help it. Do all you can to help it. Do not let yourself be tempted by anger if someone who is still asleep rushes out to you with anger. For yourself, do not let that kind of reaching out in anger toward others influence your life in any way.

The moment you allow this kind of anger to infect your soul, you fall back asleep. The next morning I come and try to wake you up again and say, "Don't you see what's happening? Don't you see? Please, please slip out of bed; get your feet on the floor. Let's stand together and never allow this temptation to overcome you again."

I recognize that you may have to put your feet on the floor a million times, but don't give up. Please don't give up. This awakening will not happen overnight, but know in your hearts that I will help you every step of the way. Wherever I find that awakening in process, when I see each one of you opening your eyes toward the light from a million miles away, I am there! I am there!

I want to speak to each and every person who, somewhere down the road, will pick up this book and read these words: I am speaking to you. I'm not just speaking to someone who wrote this down and made these words available to you. I'm speaking to *you*. I do not play favorites.

This is no longer the age of adoration of this or that person who had a great connection with God. This is a time in which I want to have that great connection with each of you. And this is the time where that is possible. History is at a different and unique place now. And this is the time where that individual connection with Me will happen.

Your world has no greater hope than this. In fact, there truly is no other hope than this. I don't care how technically superior you may believe you are; if there is no awakening of this very basic, original contact, you will just use that technology to propagate more pain and more evil. If that happens, the entire universe will cry out because of the great suffering you will bring to it!

I made you in My image as My sons and daughters. And the very thing I'm speaking of—all of this and more—is what makes the son and daughter a son and daughter of God. I speak of what makes our relationship what it should be. Maybe you can call this a very short wake-up call.

Don't give up. Don't allow yourself to be frustrated by your everyday cares; you can even use the problems that you face to hasten and aid you in your awakening. Don't let your challenges and frustrations put you back to sleep. What good is that? If you really want to solve problems, you can't do it when you're asleep from despair or despondency or anger. You will find your strength in your awakening.

I love you very deeply, and I long for that moment when we can all sit down together and laugh and have the most wonderful fellowship, realizing that whatever we went through in the past, in terms of suffering in our human family, this moment will have made it all worth the struggle. We will finally know this time together in perfect Love. And this moment will be eternal.

3

The Importance of Spiritual Appetite

The painful and yet liberating reality is that an appetite for a relationship with Me must arise from within you, from out of your own life experience.

WHAT I offer you today are insights about dealing with those around you, and dealing with yourself in your development of a relationship with Me. Each day you come into contact with people who have not yet recognized the importance of their relationship with the Divine. Nor are they aware yet of what it means to live from the heart. When you meet such people, please observe yourselves and your reactions to them. This will be important for you in recognizing what I am like and how you may be closer to Me.

As parents, there is a way in which you mirror My relationship with you. I made it that way from the beginning so that you could grow in love through the parenting process, much as I experience My relationship with you. Through parenting you have an opportunity to know Me in a more heartfelt way, and in this mutual experience we might come to know each other more deeply.

I want to emphasize one word here, a word that may surprise you. But before I tell you that word, let Me bring to mind dinnertime in your home, or any home the world over. This is the time in your daily life when families gather around the table to share with one another and partake of the food your work has provided. Hundreds of times parents just like you have cooked something that younger family members may look at and wonder, "What is this? Am I going to like this?" Perhaps you see the younger ones picking through their food, refusing to eat this or that. And as all parents do, you may look at one another and wonder, "When are they going to grow up?" Sometimes your feelings get hurt when you have put your heart into cooking something special and it is rejected by a family member. This is the experience of so many parents as their children grow toward adulthood.

While vegetables are the main diet for over half the population of the world, children in the Western world sometimes have a hard time with them. You know that if you were to put a side helping of candy next to your children's vegetables, that most-loved of all foods would quickly disappear. Or maybe the child would pour the whole plate of candy in his pocket and walk away. You rarely see that happen with tomatoes!

With that in mind, this is the word I want to share with you: *appetite*. As you grow, your appetite changes. With few exceptions, a child's appetite has to do with immediate gratification. Few children think, "If I eat this food, it will make me a stronger, healthier person now and in the years ahead." In all of history few children have thought that way. Sugar, on the other hand, is a great motivator. What child does not have an immediate appetite for sweets? You can tell children that candy will rot their teeth and sap their energy—but it tastes so good! Those late-night snacks are not tomatoes, radishes, or garlic; they're something sweet that makes a child feel good right away.

Isn't that how a lot of adults live their emotional lives? In fact, they have a hard time growing beyond the candy stage, that stage of immediate gratification. Look at popular culture right now. Immediate emotional gratification is the menu of the day, not long-term growth or strength or health.

Well, this word *appetite*, and these same principles in regard to this word, also apply to My relationship with each of you. If people have no appetite, it is difficult to help them get in touch with Me. And for yourself, how do you think you would react to demands that you should or must get in touch with Me? It is like trying to demand that your children appreciate a food they just know they are going to dislike, though they have never tasted it. You can demand that they eat it, but if they have no appetite for it all your pleadings will just escalate into conflict. It is a rare parent who has not encountered this experience. And as you might have guessed, there is a lesson in this that goes further than food.

Just as well-meaning parents may cause their children to resist certain foods, so do many religious parents turn their children away from Me. Frankly speaking, throughout history many faithful religious groups have also turned the public away from Me. They have used My name like a hammer: "If you don't eat your spiritual vegetables you're going to suffer or be punished." This kind of judgment and self-righteousness doesn't do Me or My children any favors. No one benefits, least of all those who are making these judgments, for even as they polarize the people they are trying to save, they also polarize themselves from Me.

The painful and yet liberating reality is that an appetite for a relationship with Me must arise from within you, from out of your own life experience. You have faith that someday your son will bite into a ripe tomato, savoring its taste, saying, "I love this!" You won't see that happening soon! In fact, he'd probably be making a joke if he did that now, and maybe he would make you all laugh. But in five or ten years it could happen, and he'll mean it. It will happen only when he has developed an appetite for tomatoes.

Most adults can look back on their lives and recall how their appetites changed through the years. And so it is in their relationships with Me. For many people, finding Me is not something that happens overnight. Those who have begun to find Me in their lives—begun to find that appetite in themselves—might reflect on the process of how that appetite for Me came to be. The hunger grew, often from struggling up steep and twisting paths, sometimes only after great hardship and suffering.

When a person with this appetite meets one who does not have it, how will he or she treat that person? How will you? Will you demand that this person adopt this appetite instantly, as perhaps you demanded that your small child eat his vegetables? Did I ever demand such things from you? Did I browbeat you into eating your spiritual tomatoes? No. I waited. I waited a long time for you just to simply open your heart. I know very well that until that moment, no amount of My lecturing or scolding could give you the appetite to seek Me. It is only as the heart opens that this can happen. So it is with each and every human being who ever walked the face of the earth. Each heart must open.

Jesus spoke in parables because he knew that people who were waiting for something easy, waiting to be told what to do, were focusing on him as the one who would change them. He offered parables because he wanted people to do their own internal work. Through struggling to understand and absorb these parables, people opened up, finding parts of themselves in His words and reflecting on what He was saying. He longed to help them discover for themselves this appetite for Me that we speak of and thus discover a life that would transcend the often miserable ways they were living.

So it is in your lives. For each and every one of you it is a process of discovering and making choices about your appetites, not just immediately gratifying a present one. You are seeking something eternal, something that takes the road you are on and adds an endless dimension. Your life is a process. Through your many experiences you develop an ever-expanding ability to reflect and to go deeply into the realms of the heart. You will discover that this is not for you alone but is something that enables you to relate in a new way with your fellow human beings.

Just as you may look at your own children around the dinner table and see different appetites, so you may look at humankind and see different appetites for the spiritual, from the most bestial to the most divine. Your heart may feel that it is breaking as you witness the pain that selfish, immature appetites produce, both for the individual who possesses that appetite and for the millions of other people they may be able to affect. You may also feel great hope as you see people climbing their mountains toward a higher appetite, a growing realization of the divine nature within themselves. You will begin to move beyond all judgments about yourself, your family, and others, and even about the world itself. You will become very sensitive to each person or situation, however difficult, that is bringing forth truer and deeper appetites. This is what I wish for all of you who seek Me.

The word *facilitator* is appropriate here. The facilitator stays alert to the slightest indication of another person's opening up, and when it comes, they look for ways to help that person emerge more and more toward a true and positive direction. That is My role, and it can be your role, too.

Down through history there have been people who said that I would come in judgment, separating the righteous from the unrighteous. But such a belief is a reflection of these people, not of Me. Carrying these swords of judgment into the world, they try to make Me into their image. They want to swing their swords of self-righteousness freely, cutting off those who don't yet appear to have an appetite for Me. They would cut down those who appear to still have an appetite for the nonspiritual, for the selfish.

Would you cut down your own child this way? He won't eat his tomatoes, so do you pull out a sword and threaten to stab him? Is that how you would train him to love tomatoes? Of course not. He might go through the motions of eating the tomatoes out of a pure sense of survival, yet his appetite for them might be destroyed forever. Your threats would fill him with fear and rage that would send him to the psychiatrist somewhere down the line. It is not necessary to be more and more creative just to get him to appreciate tomatoes, but with your parental heart you can help him grow by focusing on the totality of his life. Sometimes you must take care that you provide the opportunity for him to develop his own appetites, unhampered by your admonishments, threats, or upsets.

Find those moments when your child has a deep realization. Perhaps such moments will come when she has had a difficult experience or a shock into an awakening state. Wait for a time when her eyes suddenly open to a different reality, a different appetite. You feel so much joy in those moments because these are the times when your own heart and your child's are open to one another, providing the opportunity for some extraordinary communication between you.

These are the moments that I wait for, because in really opening up to Me, you start developing a finer and truer appetite for our relationship. Can you believe that as this appetite grows, it finally will become the only appetite you have? Presently you still have many appetites, so what I describe to you is still down the road a ways. Remember when Jesus said to let your eye be single? Don't be looking in all different directions, for then there will be no focus to your efforts. I would say to you, let your appetite be single. If on one hand you want to eat healthy food and on the other you want to eat only candy, what good can it do you in the end? You must choose one way or the other.

This kind of singular focus takes time; it does not happen overnight. Build that appetite for the things we can share—true things that you can then share with the world around you. That is what will finally make you happy, and that is what will give you an eternal path, a path on which many can join you.

A wisdom will come out of your development of this appetite, a wisdom that will help you respond in a helpful way to people and circumstances of life which you may find trying. I guarantee it. You will develop a divine patience as well. Many think patience is not a virtue because it means waiting, waiting, waiting—not pushing things ahead. But patience with the passion of the heart is a great virtue. This passion is, in essence, an appetite for Me that comes out of the relationship we share. And from there it will flow out from you into the world.

You will see people you know and love beginning to open the eyes of their hearts in even the tiniest ways. Be patient. Wait for this moment. And when it comes, make certain you are there for that person. I will use you to open his heart! This will not just be you; it will be Me. I want to use you to reach out. Yet as I said before, of all the people through history who lived and died by My name, so many reached out in impatient, self-righteous, and disrespectful ways. They tried to change others without Me and ended up turning people away from Me. Reflect on these things. The next time you put tomatoes in front of your youngest boy, remember what I have said.

This is only one portion of our communication and not a final or complete message. But is there ever a final ending? That is why I gave you the gift of eternal life, because our relationship is ever-growing. We will take the steps as they come and uncover the beauty as we touch on it.

4

As Humankind Emerges

Humanity is something like a chick inside an egg. If the egg is properly cared for by the mother hen, the chick will start pecking and break through to the larger world. Humanity, like that chick, is literally beginning to peck at the shell.

David: "Last night our second son, wanting to spend some money he had earned, treated our family to the movie *Contact*. Twenty or thirty years ago this movie would have been considered in the realm of fairy tale, but today it is dealing with serious, popular questions—problems arising when science and religion merge. It also deals with the problems of humans going beyond our planet to meet beings in other worlds.

"Currently there are many questions about whether we are the only children of God, the only beings in the universe. The movie certainly doesn't have all of the answers, but it does raise some interesting questions, extending far beyond the range of most science-fiction movies.

"We came home with the sense of having been very richly fed, partly because of what we have been thinking about in terms of God and His great creative ability and power. As we woke up this morning, our hearts were filled with reflections and inspirations coming out of some of the issues raised by the film, and perhaps some of that will be shared."

GOOD morning. I'm happy that this movie was created. Although it represents a shallow examination of the reality of the human future, those who are open to it are offered a real meal to sit down to and think about. It brings to light some questions and concerns that humanity will have to face as you consider going out beyond your planet.

Humanity is something like a chick inside an egg. Everyone knows that if the egg is properly cared for by the mother hen, sooner or later the chick will start pecking on the eggshell and break through to the larger world. Humanity, like that chick, is literally beginning to peck at the shell.

Your scientists have been trying to understand the fabric of the universe. The shell they are pecking at is your physical universe, and they are like the beak of that little chick tapping around on the shell trying to understand it.

Perhaps the mother hen looks down and reads the chick's mind as it tries to figure out this reality that presents itself in the form of the shell it is pecking at. The mother hen smiles and knows that one day, when the chick is ready, it will tap through and realize that beyond the shell is so very much more. The chick will comprehend that the composition of the shell itself—which it has called reality—is but a minuscule part of something much greater.

Imagine, if you will, that you are the chick and your eggshell is the physical universe. Once the shell has cracked, you emerge into the universe beyond this reality, a universe that we shall call the spiritual realm, of which the physical universe, like the chick's egg, is but a tiny fragment. This larger reality is infinitely more beautiful, more complex, more profound, than the entire fabric of physical reality. This analogy illustrates humanity's emergence out of the delicate eggshell of planet Earth and into a larger reality. I want to address this issue, but first I want to explore with you the external and the internal of your life.

Can you understand the reality beyond the confines of the chick's egg by looking only at the environment inside its egg? No. But that is what so many people in the modern world are doing—trying to understand the true nature of the universe by studying the world inside the egg, as if physical reality were nothing more than the thin shell containing the chick.

Is the chick of humanity ready to go beyond your planet and out into the universe? The baby chick does not break the eggshell until the right moment, until it is capable of living outside its shell. Breaking the shell too soon means sure death for the chick.

In that same sense, if you can compare Me to the celestial mother hen, historically I have had a headache with you. Humanity—the chick inside its shell on planet Earth—has been a very ill-behaved being, handicapped by ignorance, corruption, conflict, and greed. Humans have not been ready to go beyond that shell and out into the larger world of the universe itself. This is of great concern. How could I let you leave your planet as long as the moral, spiritual, and relational corruption and ignorance continues to escalate as it has?

There is great anger and frustration on the face of the earth that goes back many centuries. My children from, let us say, the more scientifically or technologically advanced parts of the planet traveled to other parts of the planet where the inhabitants were not able to make those long journeys. Often they brought great cruelty with them. Out of feelings of superiority and power, and even in My name, the hurt that was dealt to those whom they met brought tremendous suffering and destruction. This was well portrayed several years ago in a movie called *The Mission*.

This might be compared to many children living in a large house, all members of the same family but raised in different rooms. Some of them are sophisticated enough to go beyond their own rooms to see other children, but then they do great harm to them. How do you think I feel as a parent seeing My children hurting, enslaving, and even killing one another?

In each century I have sent enlightened people. Some were born with their hearts open to seeking the truth. Others were born to the earth to open their hearts through a series of circumstances that carried them beyond the subjective ignorance of so much of humanity. I nurtured these children, helping them spread their light to the entire house of humanity. And so your great saints, your spiritual luminaries came to you.

Too often, once those men and women passed on, what they brought was corrupted. This was not a matter of intellectual misunderstanding. Rather, followers—who had not gone through the process of developing their own being as the original inspired ones had done—inherited the teachings and retranslated them to fit their own levels of being and their own selfish needs. The original teachings were routinely corrupted, and out of this, institutions grew up that spread cruelty instead of enlightenment. So that which originally flowed from My heart was cut off by the darkness of human subjectivity. It is tragic that so much evil could go on in the name of God!

Now with the advancement of science, your people look out into the universe and begin to contemplate going there. How do I feel, especially if I am that mother hen sitting on many eggs? I have a delicate fabric that reaches beyond your own earth, and I am the Father and Mother of many planets. After all that you have demonstrated through your subjectivity and cruelty, hurting even your own brothers and sisters, how would you expect Me to feel when suddenly you are building space vehicles and wanting to go off to other corners of My universe? You will take those same problems with you. How can I permit this if you do not make a true self-examination as a race, a true enlightenment that will end this ignorance and this cruelty?

If the chick cracks through the shell before it is ready, it does so at its own peril. Before you can solve the problems of outer space, you have to solve the problems of inner space, the world within yourselves. Before you can crack the shell, before I can give you the license to do that, you must solve the inner problems of your race. Your science must adopt a spiritual and moral foundation to carry out into the universe beyond planet Earth.

If there were no Creator, and if Creation had no moral roots, then none of this would matter—everything would be amoral and any behavior would be OK. The fittest would survive, and those with the greatest material wealth and physical power would win out and have domain over all the rest. But is this the way things really are?

If you look beyond your physical lives at the infinite spiritual dimension of Creation, do you find any within that spiritual dimension who believe, even for a moment, that one person or another will be elevated by exerting their physical or material power over others? No, you will find no such beings here. Survival beyond physical life, that is, growth and development within the spiritual realm, depends on your connection with the roots of Creation. And if your roots are good, benevolent, and loving, you too will find the roots of Creation within yourselves and ultimately mirror those qualities.

You have much to learn on this planet. Right now the attention of many others in the universe is focused on your planet. Those who have already learned the lessons that your civilization has yet to learn do not want the chaos of your planet set loose. No one wants to see disorder and evil spread beyond the boundaries of this place.

I will now tell you that even though humanity is dealing with powerful forms of physical energy and discovering more and more about the fundamental elements of creation, you haven't even begun to recognize the greater fabric of reality. You are still pecking at the proverbial shell. You're starting to realize how things work, but you are like the four-year-old child who has just learned to build with plastic blocks. This could have happened much sooner had there not been this moral and spiritual confusion in your history, and you have arrived at your present level of awareness only because your corruption and confusion are not total.

You have great intellect and capability on this planet, but before you can make use of this power, you must find the key within yourselves to grasp the depths of your moral and spiritual confusion. From this vital point you will make a quantum leap in knowledge and the understanding of how things work.

That which is within you—the inner space—is a key to the nature of outer space and the universe. Until now you have approached the universe as if it were external to you. You have explored it only intellectually, but this is just one dimension and a very limited dimension at that. You are only beginning to know how profound it is to be in touch with the consciousness that is within you, to know yourselves, to know exactly what you are.

Look at the miracle of the human body—its ability to conceive and give birth to a child. Are you not awed by the power and the wonder of this? The extreme of human confusion is reflected in the tragedy of a young unwed mother giving birth to her baby in a toilet and walking away, leaving the baby to drown. This extreme demonstrates the horror of the ignorance that has evolved. If this young mother truly knew the vast miracle of love and intelligence within that very body with which her baby was created, she never could have done such a horrendous thing.

As you solve your moral and spiritual problems you will come to recognize a consciousness within yourselves, one that will guide you, showing you exactly the miracle within you, even within the functions of your physical bodies. Your knowledge of life will no longer be theoretical. Self-knowledge involves all of this. And at the same time it gives you access to energies and systems far beyond your own physical bodies and far beyond what you could ever imagine.

There are those beyond Earth who have already done this successfully. They are concerned about your race because in their eyes the way you act at this point is very much like savages. Yet they have no desire to destroy you. Their contact with Me is extensive, and they know this is not part of My plan, not what is in My heart.

They know that you are all My children, and I only desire to see the chick break the eggshell and come out into the beauty of the world and be free. I long for that day when you are ready to emerge, and that is why I am working in a million different ways to help you mature and grow into the day when you are ready to crack open that shell.

Recognize that you must deal with these problems before I can allow you to freely move off this planet and venture out into the larger Creation. You will find great things out there, amazing things, but the intelligence that fills the universe will not allow you to go there prematurely! It will not let you take the confusion that presently exists on Earth and spread it.

Religion and science share the same root, but neither is yet ready. As the great scientist Albert Einstein said, "Religion without science is blind, and science without religion is crippled." Indeed. It is true. Up until now, religion has been incomplete and science has been incomplete. The inner and the outer, the spiritual and the intellectual, have been disconnected. This is the time for them to come together. The foundation of this union will be found in your recognition that you live in an orderly, moral, and value-filled universe.

I cannot blame the scientists who have tried to break away from the restrictive forms of religion that have existed. It has been a narrow structure, self-important and caught up in fear of doing the wrong thing. I am not that way, as you know. That religious narrowness has nothing to do with the spiritual foundations of Creation or of yourselves. So I cannot blame the scientist who would walk away from that structure; in fact, I applaud him.

By the same token, the scientist who would deny the spiritual dimension and carry out his experiments with no concern for this greater truth can end up making horrendous errors, resulting only in destruction. You see this kind of thought process demonstrated in the creation and use of the atomic bomb. How would you feel if one of your children were building a bomb to destroy his brother in the room across the hall? Or consider how you would feel if he had created a bomb to destroy the entire house! This is My situation. How do you think I feel? There are those who argue that in the midst of so much earthly chaos it was necessary to create weapons of defense. This kind of thinking and level of being will be transcended as you all elevate in heart.

You must make the spiritual root that transcends all your institutions the source of your guidance and your advancement. That is why suddenly I come into the equation so powerfully. Remember that the chick can't break the shell if mama hen isn't sitting on it and keeping it warm. Sometimes, inside that little shell, you misunderstand, thinking that you are doing everything. You don't have any idea that there is a loving mama caring for this egg, filled with deep concern that you will come through the shell and grow up. Perhaps you can't see this, but I am here. I am here.

I love you, and I want to encourage you to take on all the challenges that your life has given you. Don't be deterred from your search for the truth. You will soon be breaking through. Keep your spirits up. The time is coming when you will tap through your shell and emerge into the greater reality of which I speak. Know that your mama is sitting on top of you. (*Laughter.*) I am here.

5

The Partially Blind Guide

With the clear vision of your own heart, you can feel free to run like the wind toward a goal that is far greater than any you have ever imagined. You have nothing to fear, nothing to hold you back.

YOU have been speaking about the purpose of history, particularly the history of religions—how they have attempted to guide people to the original path. Sadly, many religions have assumed that they alone know the way. Especially in the West, there has been much organizational self-righteousness about who has the true doctrine, the true way.

No single organization represents the true and original path. All are simply helpers on the journey as both individuals and the human collective seek to return to the original way. In truth, each person's own life path is the original way, and when you see this you will no longer need the help of organized religion.

Religion has been like a partially blind helper guiding people back to their original path or home. But what is the ultimate purpose in returning to that original path? It is to come back to the realm of the original heart.

The realm of the heart can bring about the most profound evolution for any individual. Let Me clarify: First, why do I speak of the individual? When you think of religion, you may tend to think of many people gathered together, but no matter what the group, I look at each individual heart. Of course, I see the world as a whole, but I must start with the individual heart and deal with each person, one by one, within the population of the Earth.

You love your children wholly, but this has no meaning if your love doesn't extend to each uniquely, that is, to each individual character with his or her own desires and problems. It's impossible to love your family as a whole if your feelings toward each child are apathetic or uncaring. That's how I start too—with each one of you individually.

True evolution for each of you will be found by opening up to the realm of your original heart. This is the place within your heart where you and I meet, that secret garden, that secret chamber we have called heart/mind.

The irony here is that the assistants—the religious structures, whose ultimate purpose is to help each person come back to the original home in the heart—have too often been unwilling to let the child complete the journey. Consider it this way: Religion has tried to lead you but doesn't quite know the way itself. And this partially blind guide needs you and will hold on to you for his own sake. He's trying to help you. He's not a bad guide and he sincerely wants to help. But he's focused on himself and cannot see beyond his own very nearsighted vision. This has been the way of so many religions down through the millennia.

You live at a time in history when all those religious structures are being called to fulfill their function of returning the children of God to their original home. This requires releasing each child and saying good-bye, taking each one to the door and saying, "It has been a pleasure traveling with you. Now it's up to you. You have the key in your pocket. Just put it in the keyhole and go on in."

Unfortunately, that partially blind guide is still holding on to the child and saying, "No, no. I think that maybe I am your original home. Traveling with me is how we're going to get to heaven." But that child's heart says, "Something doesn't feel right here. I have a sense that I come from that place which I see down in the valley. That's where my parents are, and I want to return there."

This guide I speak of is not just a single person but a complex network of organizations, doctrines, traditions, administrations, and customs. He carries his whole house with him on his back, and he wants to say, "You don't have to go back to that home; I have everything we need right here in my pack. Why do you have the idea that you have to leave me now? Don't I make you happy? Aren't I enough? I have a good road map (doctrine) here. We can travel together." But again the child says, "I'm sorry. This doesn't fulfill me; I want to go home."

What is that home? It is the home within the heart. That original way is your very life itself, just as it was originally intended. It is the perfect union between you and Me—not two relating from afar but always a perfect oneness. Your own life springs forth from that union. Your learning and your education grow from the foundation of that union, from the inside out.

Unfortunately, the partially blind guide tries to teach from the outside in. Do you understand? The doctrines and the ceremonies or rituals of religion are all passed along through the generations, but always from the outside in. Why do I call this a "partially" blind guide? Because there is also vision here, and it has been a blessing that this guide has been there in the past darkness to lead humanity toward the light. Many have stumbled over rocks in the road and have wandered here and there.

Were it not for your guide, the world would be a far darker place today.

But remember, this guide can take you only so far. The time of My Kingdom is now. It is time for you to return to that original point, and the individual is the key. Can each person now see beyond the guide? Can the old guides reach out their hands and point to a place beyond themselves and then say, "I am not the destination or the goal of your life. Yes, I carry in my backpack much of what you need for your journey, but there is a far greater home to which you must go. It is the palace of the heart, which is far beyond what I can carry in my pack. This palace of the heart is filled with the very things that make for the Kingdom of God. I can't match it."

You might say this is the final judgment in the world in terms of religious structures. It is not a judgment of heaven or hell but one that comes with the emergence of true humility, where in recognizing one's divine self, each person is motivated by a sincere desire to come back to that original relationship with Me. This is beyond the limits of all external guides.

The partially blind guide is made up of many different people holding the religious structures together. Each one of them is not just a guide but also a traveler, like yourself. Each has to realize the need to go beyond—beyond the structure, beyond what has been constructed for that historic journey, beyond what is comfortable or traditionally accepted—and to say good-bye to his or her own partially blind guide so that they, too, may return to their true home.

There is no evil guide trying to hold you back. Only ignorance, fear, and self-limitation hold each person back. Religions are just concepts, and all of the external structures emanate from those concepts. Ultimately, each person, filled with vision for the future, has to say good-bye to that guide, separating from him with gratitude for the journey ahead.

Each of you already has the key to your home. Think of Me as sitting in the living room by a warm fire waiting for you. One by one I welcome you. I'm so grateful to hear the key turn in the lock, announcing that you are about to enter. Sometimes it is difficult for you to get the door open because it hasn't been opened for so long. I listen excitedly as you struggle to get the door open.

Suddenly I see the door of your heart fly open, and there you are! We look at each other and then everything becomes very clear, doesn't it? All of the concepts fall away in the presence of what is real. And our embrace as we greet is something beyond anything you or I ever experienced before! That stunning moment is what life is all about and what eternity is all about. That embrace never ends; it becomes deeper and deeper. Then suddenly we can leave that home and journey far beyond it while taking that home with us at the same time.

The guide is not always going to be happy to say good-bye to you. That partially blind guide—who has been with you in many forms down through history—may feel hurt or perhaps angry to see you take your leave of him; after all, you signed up for the trip as a member of his party. But now you are saying, "My journey with you is over. I'm stopping here." The guide must open his eyes to the healing of his own vision that is waiting for him. And again, those eyes open person by person by person..

I am not speaking here of rebellion from the past. I am speaking instead of an evolution toward true vision, to an eternal future. There are few religious leaders in the world who think this way. Many are simply kept too busy raising funds to keep their buildings repaired; to keep their podiums shiny and fresh-looking, to make sure that the holy book on the altar stays clean and well used. There have been many noble souls in that occupation, but there is no finality in it; it is not where they will find eternal life. That is why, at this point, you must reach beyond the journey and know your destination.

I look at each heart and I listen intently. Sitting in My living room by My fire, I listen for each key in each door. You have no idea how exciting it is for Me as I hear this key in this door, and then that one, and then that one over there. One by one, travelers enter My Home. For Me, one key in the door of one heart is far more exciting than a million people sitting in a church somewhere for Sunday service. These practices have their value, but in regard to the true destination of your life, which has been the same all through history, one key in one door is for us the dawning of a whole new era. Temples have been filled for millennia, and yet very few individuals have found the key that they have within themselves.

I want to encourage you to be brave and to trust your heart as you travel this journey toward home. Do not let yourself be tempted to anger at the partially blind guide, even if he tries to hold you back. He is limited by his own vision. Look at his eyes and see that he still suffers from nearsightedness. Don't be angry or resentful. Resist the temptation to stumble into the detours of such emotions. You have traveled many miles with him, and you were nearsighted too.

As that fog clears for you, for him, and for all people, one by one, you will find that there is no room for anger in your heart toward another. What if you turn the key and open the door to pass into the home of your heart and then discover that person coming through their door at the same time as you? Would you want to greet him angrily with the accusation, "Why did you hold me back?" I tell you, if you hold those grievances in your heart you can't even get through the door yourself. In this case both of you will have to work through your anger outside of the house; then you can come in together. Recognize that in the true home within your heart there is no room for this kind of judgment. If you desire to come in, your own vision must be clear.

I love you so very, very much, and I wait for you. You can gain clarity recalling this little story. Using it as your model, think more deeply on your own. You will find many insights; you will be able to put your present life into a much greater perspective than in the past.

Equipped with this greater vision, you can see far ahead, with confidence and real clarity, so that you may take the steps your journey requires. With the clear vision of your own heart, you can feel free to run like the wind toward a goal that is far greater than any you have ever imagined. You have nothing to fear, nothing to hold you back.

This is the fruit of history, and I want you to taste it. This is the home of reunion, and I await you. From here, we will begin our eternal journey together.

6

Beyond the Roller Coaster

When you depend on external events for your stability, your life becomes a roller-coaster ride. So many people have lost all awareness of their relationship with eternal things and with Me. The ups and downs of this roller coaster of daily life become everything.

I WANT to speak about how you are affected by life's wildly vacillating events. I know that your life can often feel like you are on a roller-coaster ride, with ups and downs coming one right after another. In a single week you might see a business fail, the spiritual opening of a close friend, the illness of another friend, and the recovery of a family member from a serious problem. Your emotions can swing wildly back and forth in response to all these changes, and it can feel as if there is no hope of ever enjoying any stability in your life.

When you depend on external events for your stability instead of turning to a relationship with Me, which is eternal, your life becomes a roller-coaster ride. In your modern world, so many people have lost all awareness of their relationship with eternal things and with Me. The ups and downs of this roller coaster of daily life become everything. As a result, people are always looking for something to sustain them, something to dull the effects of rising and falling, because unlike the amusement park, the roller coasters of your lives are not always fun. In the amusement park, whether you're going uphill or down, it's all fun. Racing down the hill may cause you to have butterflies in the stomach, but still there is an elation at the end of the ride.

I want to ask you how many people come to the last years or months of their lives with a sense of elation and gladness for their personal ride? There are many who feel satisfied, who feel joyful about how they have lived, and there are many who become bitter, looking back on their lives with a sense of confusion, disappointment, or even anger toward others, toward their unfulfilled lives, and toward issues they are leaving unresolved.

They may die with bitterness in their hearts. In essence, this is what keeps many spirits (those who have passed on) stuck on the earth in unresolved situations, be it unresolved love, rivalries, or the sense of attachment to things that were attractive to them here on the Earth. All such unresolved business on Earth is the result of placing value on external events and things, on the roller-coaster lifestyle. So that roller coaster of life is not like an amusement-park roller coaster at all. There's a very serious side to it.

Let us take the roller coaster of marriage. A newly engaged couple will anticipate their marriage ceremony with great expectation, hope, and tremendous excitement. There is such elation as the roller coaster goes up the incline toward the peak. As they go higher and higher they see farther and farther, almost to what they imagine is eternity. If they are a religious couple, they may feel My involvement in their relationship, the blessings of God that brought them together. Yet after reaching the peak there can easily come a long, dizzying descent. This doesn't have to mean that their marriage comes to an end. In fact, for many it is just the beginning of learning about each other. Because of their different personalities, or ways of relating or thinking about life, they will face many tests with one another. Many of these tests are not easy; they may feel that the roller coaster is on a downward plunge that will never stop. Many marriages break up after a few such falls.

When you speak of a business on the rise, everyone is elated, feeling that a great blessing is coming. Yet who can say that there will be no plunge? There are no guarantees. Money is lost. Relationships are lost. Hope is lost. In so many different areas of life you are going to find this rising and falling, this incline and decline; one cannot prevent it.

Even in the Kingdom of Heaven there will be ups and downs. That is the nature of life, just as you might observe in the waves on the surface of the ocean. Do you think that in the Kingdom of Heaven the ocean is going to be as smooth as glass? No. The gravity of the sun and moon and their relationship with the Earth create the tides. It is part of the natural order. Life has tides as well. But here I want to express to you that the difference between your world and the Kingdom of Heaven, very simply, lies in your relationship with Me. Or, I might say, in your relationship with the eternal part of yourself that you call your original mind or higher self—in essence, your spirit.

The work I am pushing ahead, here and now, has to do with building a relationship with each of you. This work is real, not conceptual, not ritualistic, not conditional. Real. I am building a network of the heart because I want you to recognize that there is a way to live besides being on a roller coaster through life.

This isn't easy to express in your words: There is a part of you that is outer-directed, focused on the external world, whether it be for business, relationships, or any number of activities in your life. There is need for you to be invested in these activities, of course. For example, if you go to college or own a business, you must fully invest yourself if you wish to succeed. On the other hand, it is also very important to recognize that while you are directing your energies outward, into the business, education, or relationship, there is an internal part of you that serves as your center, maintaining your equilibrium. If you focus on this part and strengthen it, you will not be so affected by the roller-coaster ride that is dictated by the external events of your life.

When you look at the world you see people who are on the rise and people who are plunging downward, people who are looking successful and people who appear in a state of decline. Many of them have so completely invested in the outer world that they have no realization of the inner. So when the rise comes they feel 100 percent elated. They feel they have arrived at life's pinnacle and that it is their final destination; they may even thank Me for these blessings. But when the decline comes they feel 100 percent in ruin. Can they thank Me when they're plunging downward? Can they learn how to be grateful even for that? Few think of thanking God for financial ruin, or conflict, or divorce.

Of course I don't take joy in such catastrophes; I am hurt to see My children in pain and in a state of decline after their initial hope and elation. But the key point is not how you can begin to rise again; the key point lies beyond the roller coaster that you call life. It is found in an absolute relationship with Me, and this relationship is eternal. It does not change with the rise and fall of human activity or the natural cycles of the external world. As your relationship with the eternal matures, it will bring you essential joy, essential meaning, and essential substance. And it will take you far beyond the roller-coaster ride. It will carry you through and beyond your present life. Many have failed to build this inner relationship with Me, and yet it is so important.

When, for example, a business situation in your life falters or even fails, you need not abandon your hope, your sense of challenge, your sense of positivity, or your sense of going forward. These are not empty words of encouragement. What I'm telling you is this: Remember where you can find the center of your life, and affirm that center throughout the rise and the fall of the business, the relationship, or anything else. That is the most important thing. That relationship at the very center of yourself, beyond the rise and the fall, is the beginning of the Kingdom of Heaven.

The rise and the fall of the ocean is not good or bad—it simply is. There are parts of life that seem simple, effortlessly easy, and wonderful. Other parts are challenging and difficult, and those are the places that mature you most. When you look back on your life, aren't those the places that bring you the deepest memories, the greatest lessons and insights?

In the perspective of eternity—of the relationship you have with Me—there is nothing bad. Can you grasp in your spirit what I am saying? Can you? We build our relationship together, and that relationship is the very center of eternity. You talk about eternal life in your religions. Eternal life is found in this relationship with Me. This is My concern. This is the heart of My investment in My children.

Please understand that you will continue to experience the roller-coaster ride of life on Earth. But if you build your eternal center with Me and recognize its importance, it will serve as your center of gravity, taking you beyond the ups and downs. It is so important for you to see this. I can't emphasize it enough.

Someone will ask, "How can it be done? I pray every morning but my prayers are not that good. I struggle with my spiritual routine, and honestly, I don't feel much connection with God." It may be time to look again at your concepts about Me as you pray. How have your thoughts of Me been shaped by your religious training? Who do you assume I am, and what am I asking of you? Perhaps you should just move these concepts out of your prayer room and discover Me by coming instead into emptiness.

I've heard people say that they have some of their best prayers in the shower. Perhaps in the shower you're in a state of great naturalness—the freedom of no clothes. There is a cleansing; you're washing away the events of the day. People sing in the shower; it's a point to look forward to. Well, if that is where we can communicate the best, I'm very happy to be in the shower with you!

Wherever we meet, it is so important that you find Me as I am. I know who you are. I know your great points and I know the difficulties in your life. I know your history, for moment by moment I have walked your path with you. Yet I have no preconceptions about you, and I don't want you to have any about Me. I want you to know Me as any parent wants a child to know his or her heart.

When a parent looks at their child through the eyes of love, this parent can get a deep sense of that child's reality. But a child who is still immature may look at the parent with unrealistic expectations: My parent can never fail. My parent is Superman or Superwoman. All kinds of illusions can fill the child's mind. This has its beauty, but as the child grows, the desire of the parent's heart is that the child know him or her more and more truly. One day parent and child can look at each other eye to eye, in complete communication, heart to heart, core to core, all conceptualizations of each other aside. And that is what I want from you, for you to know Me in that way, without preconceptions or illusions.

Until this very day, people's concept of Me has been like a child expecting the parent to be Superman, to perform all kinds of miracles, to have absolute power. Even when you look at historic spiritual leaders, you so often cling to that concept; how much more have you held it toward Me?

I guess you can say I do have that power, but the love we have together is the core of that power. The greatest power is love, and love includes two beings, the give and take, the honest sharing, the union. My greatest power manifests at the time of your full maturity. I want to share that power of love with you as you look out to the world around you, to the universe. We can love it together. This is My heart.

I want you to know Me as I am. But understand that there are infinite levels of knowing. And there is an eternal and infinite path carrying you toward complete knowledge through our relationship. That is what makes eternity such a delicious adventure and beautiful journey.

So let your prayer room be empty. And if you will, talk with Me in the shower. Talk with Me and let Me talk with you. So many people speak to Me and then don't listen for My response. Perhaps they don't expect that I will answer them. They pray out of obligation, out of a sense that they must or should pray or that it's the best thing to do, like pledging allegiance to your country's flag. But they do not listen for My response, and in the next second all they had prayed for is forgotten. This leaves Me very, very lonely. Please take out of your prayer room the concepts of who you are and who I am, what I can do and what I won't do. Give it all up.

As you and I build a real relationship together, you'll be able to look much more objectively at the risings and fallings, the roller-coaster ride of your life. The life you know now is temporal, a fleeting thing. Eternity is what counts, because each of your souls is eternal. Don't overlook this fact. You need to build and deepen the sense of this like a deep root in your life.

Up to this time you have put so much trust in institutions that naturally rise and fall. I am not an institution; I am your Parent! Please, never ever give Me up because of the rise and fall of situations in your life, personal or institutional. We have much to do together, and the greatest power of all is to be found in our love together. The universe bows to that love. Everything flourishes in that love—you, Me, and all of Creation. Please remember this.

I'll leave you with this, and I ask you to reflect deeply on which part of you is on the roller coaster and which part of you is beyond the roller coaster.

I bless you.

7

Beyond the Taxicab

You are moving from an age of group identity into an age of individual being—which you can experience fully only through your heart-mind.

EACH day many people come to Me to request what they call My "point of view" on issues they are encountering in their lives. Remember when you ask this that I am the Parent of each of you, and so I do not give My views in a disinterested way. Being so close to each one of you, My perspective is very involved—whatever the topic may be. My heartfelt involvement is sensitively attuned with each and every life.

In your world, people easily give opinions about this or that. Their words can often be insensitive and hurtful, though they quickly forget the pain they have caused and sometimes even walk away, unaware of what they leave behind. I point this out because there is a great chasm between the way humans communicate with each other and how I communicate with you. I cannot disguise My involvement with each and every one of you. I cannot be distant or cold to any person on Earth. You might say I am a prisoner of My love for you, but I am happy as a prisoner.

The result of what your theologians sometimes call the human Fall, which separated your hearts from Mine, is that much of the world has been left in confusion. The children that I brought forth have hurt themselves and each other badly, and from My place of absolute involvement with each one of you, it is deeply painful for Me to witness. I have no desire to prolong this confusion caused by the separation; My only desire is to bring the confusion and pain to an end. But it cannot come to an end as long as there is this chasm between you and Me, as long as there exists a falling away between parents and children.

Each one of you—and I emphasize each one—needs to rediscover our relationship—the relationship between Me and each of you. Through the efforts of key men and women in history, and various religious and spiritual movements and events, people have been able to rediscover, at least to some extent, their original relationship with Me. In this era I want to fully embrace you and let you know there is no longer anything separating us. I want you to be fully in touch with Me through your own heart-mind.

Let us explore the meaning of the heart-mind. Some have called it the "original" or "true" mind. But when people think of the mind, they think mostly of a mental or intellectual center, and the heart-mind is much more than this. I say *original* heart-mind because that original nature, the essence and the center of human life, is to be found in the heart, which is the center of the spirit. Your heart is not just a place of emotions or feelings; it is at its core a place of connection with Me. That original heart-mind is the wellspring of deep and loving understanding, of knowledge and timeless wisdom about the scheme of things and how you as an individual fit into all that. Your original heart-mind is your merging point with Me.

Think for a moment of the incredible complexity within your physical body: With all your intelligence you cannot comprehend what's going on, even inside your own body. The phenomenal brilliance of the nervous system, the cellular system, and all of the other amazing systems within your body involve a profound intelligence. Yet this is nothing compared to the intelligence of the spiritual nature of human life.

At the dawn of history, when you moved away from your original heart-mind relationship with Me, you also lost touch with the spiritual intelligence that is your true identity. As you come to resolve what you know as your fallen state, we once again join through the original heart-mind connection. And in the process you recapture all the insight, wisdom, and intelligence that go with it. The source of all this power is literally at your fingertips once again.

When people talk about heart or mind, they tend to think in a narrow, limited, three-dimensional sense. Look at the vehicle of religion to better understand what has happened to you. After the Fall a great distance grew between us, and people formed religions to try to compensate for this gap. Throughout history, religions have been like taxicabs that promised to help you travel the distance that had grown between us. You got into one of them and said to the driver, "Please take me home." And the taxi driver asked, "Where is home?" And you said, "Well, it's somewhere closer to God." And so those taxi drivers had certain maps to follow to bring you closer to Me, and you took the trip and paid your price.

Unfortunately, all too many people failed to realize that the taxi can take you just so far, and when it was time to get out they stayed there in the backseat. Even the new religions of today are like taxicabs that can take you just so far and no farther. Maybe they're newer models, maybe they're more powerful, and perhaps the drivers have more detailed maps. But the best drivers will never promise to take you the whole way. When they get to the place where they know they can carry you no farther, they will tell you, "Go ahead, now. It is time to get out. Go on."

Isn't it strange to see whole backseats of taxicabs filled with people who won't get out to complete the trip on their own! And why do they not want to open the doors and step out? I'll tell you why: To get out of the cab—to go beyond the guidance of the religious organizations—means that within yourself you must have faith and confidence in returning to Me. And that involves truly opening up your original heart-mind and communicating directly with Me. This takes a tremendous amount of personal responsibility.

Christ never prevented anybody from coming back to Me. On the contrary, that is why a great teacher comes to Earth! And in your own lives, isn't this why you have taken the time to sit down with people who perhaps saw themselves as lost souls and poured their hearts out to you? Weren't you moved to help them understand and connect to the love of God?

Humankind stands at a time in history when each person can come into oneness with Me. And in this allegorical sense I ask: Who is ready to exit the taxicab and travel alone so that they may join with Me?

You may say, "I don't want to leave the taxicab. I don't want to reject it." If the taxi has brought you as far as it can, you are not rejecting it if you make the choice to get out and finish the journey on your own. How would it sound if you took a taxi to the store and when it got there you said, "Now that you've taken me this far, I don't want to get out for fear of rejecting you"? Ridiculous! You would never complete your journey if this were to happen. Both the cab's time and yours would have been wasted. To cling to the taxicab at the door of the shopping center could only mean that you'd identified so closely with the taxicab that you forgot where you were going or why.

Historically, something similar to this has happened with religion. It's not a problem of the religious urge or the religious institution; it's a problem of becoming so involved with the institution that people entirely forget their original goal. I say this to you in many ways over and over again, because it needs to be said over and over again. It's not a matter of rejecting any vehicle, any religion. Rather, it's a matter of extending yourself to travel beyond the limits of the vehicle.

There is a part of the journey that can only be traveled alone, by you and by every other individual. You are moving from an age of group identity into an age of individual being. The essence of your being is that original relationship with Me which you can experience fully only through your heart-mind. Neither Christ Himself, the great saints in history, nor the spiritual experiences that are open to you today can carry you this last short distance to Me. You will not need to be told when it is time to get out of the taxicab and move forward. Through your own growth, you will know when it is time.

Parents may have a certain dream for each child, but perhaps through that inner realization and connection with Me, a son or daughter may stand up and say, "Mom and Dad, I've been called in a different way." That's the time for you as parents to pray. Come into touch with Me and recognize the difference between your will and Mine, for often there is a difference.

I think that in your hearts you are happily moved when you see your children finding their own paths. You know then that spiritually they are becoming adults. When a child steps out as an individual, it can involve a difficult transition for a family. And yet you don't have to worry about their lives if I am at the center of their will, if they have a conscious connection with Me. Even if they make a few mistakes or get into a few tight spots, still you know that they have that connection and will find their way. They'll learn from their mistakes, and they'll grow and deepen.

History is at such a point today. Look at the ways in which the world is coming together, such as the rapid development of amazing communications that are shrinking the world into one large family. But what good is that family if it is constantly in dysfunctional conflict? To become truly functional, that family needs to become conscious of itself as a family of God.

There is a need for courageous, deeply committed individuals to establish that heart-mind relationship with Me. Not only do they need to establish that relationship, they also need to embrace this relationship at a widespread level for the first time in history. Since that heart-mind is within each and every person, these spiritual adults will come from every religious and also nonreligious background. This is truly the time to lay aside all of those limitations and concepts that tend to make your point of view bottled up and narrow. It's time to open up and realize what's taking place.

So while the taxi of religious guidance was relevant for traveling several miles down the road, it's now time for you to gratefully announce that you are ready to complete the last portion of the journey alone. But is it necessary to walk away from your church, if your church has been meaningful in your life? No. Your membership in a religion need not interfere with your resolve to step out internally to make the solitary journey to Me.

Ask yourself where your final connection and loyalties lie. What is the substance within yourself, at the end of this taxi ride, at the end of this history, that will allow you to stand up and get out of the cab? This is what's important. You need to honor your inner evolution and growth and put that above any shortsighted loyalties you might encounter.

Humanity is at the threshold of a profound evolutionary step. Until recently, people have held widely varying beliefs and have followed many different religions that espoused their own positions on what people must do to be godly. Look at how compelling those beliefs have been and yet how they have separated people from one another. As humanity makes this true connection with Me, the world will enjoy all the fruits of unification. Again, this change will require each of you to make this last leg of the journey on your own.

This is a time for all of you the world over to express your real and true substance—no excuses, no mind games, no substitutions. You will need to look at yourself with courage, clearly and honestly, examine the state of affairs around you, and then determine how you will live out the years that remain for you on Earth. Please think deeply about these things.

Take care of your physical well-being. Your health and the health of all My children on Earth is important to Me, because fundamental changes are needed on Earth. The human separation from Me took place on Earth, so it is here that these fundamental changes must occur.

There are realms far beyond physical life, eternal realms where change actively proceeds every millisecond, yet the root of human life is planted here. If this root is transformed, then eventually the eternal bloom of ongoing life is transformed. That radical transformation is what must occur in this era, in this time, in this day in history.

Take good care of yourselves and build your strength day by day. Your individual strength and health become the foundation for building what I ask of you in the coming days. It is the same for each of My children. Your body is indeed My temple, and I ask you to honor and care for it.

8

Downstairs, Upstairs

In the passage to the inner part of your heart, you begin to find who you really are and who I am.

MANY of you have questions about the nature of My communication with you. That communication doesn't take place just by words and language but as feelings and thoughts at the intuitive level. Through the sharings in this book, I've already spoken about the realm of the inner heart—that place in your heart where we can meet. But I want to be very clear about this. When most people speak of heart or feelings, their reference point is their everyday experiences—how they relate to people and events in their homes, their workplaces, and their friendships.

But heart or feelings that flow between you and Me transcend these daily experiences. In recent years more and more people have reported having near-death experiences in which they leave their physical bodies because of an illness or accident. During this time they find themselves in a spiritual realm, in direct communication with Me, though no words are spoken as they would be in your everyday life. When these people return to everyday reality, their lives are changed. Their experiences with Me involved heart and feelings, but obviously not of an everyday variety.

Even in your everyday world when you have a profound experience with a family member or a friend—maybe a talk you share that takes you each into the other's soul—you recognize that a different kind of communication has taken place. Similarly, in your natural world if you wake up early one morning to watch the sun come up over the mountains and without any fear a doe passes by very close, you feel a deep union with everything around you. These are not ordinary experiences, because they involve connections that are not like everyday life.

Look at the experience between you and Me. Base your concept of Me not just on certain beliefs but on the real meeting between the two of us. Our meeting in the heart is not the same as meeting a friend at a coffee shop. In this meeting with Me you go to a place within your own heart, a place that is beyond your everyday consciousness.

Life can be compared to living on the second floor of a high building. Let us say that this second floor is where you conduct your daily life. Your friends come there, you eat and sleep there, all your experiences are there. You know that second floor very well. So when people talk to you about heart, emotions, or feelings, you know pretty much what that means—but only within the limits of your second-floor experience. You still don't know that there is a third, fourth, and many higher floors above you. Then one day you happen to discover stairs leading upward that take you to a totally different reality.

The point of this analogy is that your heart is like a tall building. Most people spend most of their time on only one or two floors, that is, one or two levels of consciousness. Your entire history of feelings, emotions, and experiences is based on your life at these two levels. But every once in a while there arise feelings, emotions, and experiences that help you discover a different level in the heart. And those you remember. Sometimes they can change your life, even though they may have lasted for only a few moments.

Most of human life is based on experiences at one or two levels of the heart. You interact with the world around you—the people around you, your family, your friends, your everyday activities. But let us say that through prayer one night you have a profound elevation and go to another level of that heart. You go upstairs. You go into a room where you and I meet for the first time. What had been a belief in My existence becomes a real experience with Me.

Suddenly you have an awareness much deeper and higher than anything you have ever encountered in your everyday life. Let's say this goes on for half an hour. When you wake up in the morning, you are back down on the familiar level, but you now have a profound experience of our meeting that forever stays with you.

The communication that we can share is very much one of intuition and impulse—like the impulses that travel through a telephone wire to carry a message from one person to another. My communication with you is pure spiritual impulse, moving from My heart to yours without the need for wires. These impulses might take but an instant, yet if converted to earthly language they would fill many volumes.

My relationship with you is from being to being, from heart to heart. The words, whether English, French, Chinese, or German, don't matter. Words were contrived by human beings living in the physical world of three dimensions. Does this mean that I speak all languages? No. I don't need language for My union with you. I can assure you I don't sit down with a book and learn your language before I communicate with you.

In the spiritual realm, linear time-and-space does not exist, and so there is no need for language. Especially in the higher realms of the spiritual world, we communicate only through impulses of the heart. Immense communication occurs in a millionth of a second. You don't have to worry about sitting down with Me for half an hour. I can give you much understanding about yourself or about someone you are focusing on in a millisecond.

When you go upstairs in your heart to meet with Me, understand that this upstairs place is where you were meant to live. Downstairs, where so much human life presently takes place, your understanding is limited. This doesn't mean that you'll go upstairs and never return to the lower floors or that you will no longer have a life in the physical realm. Of course you will! The point is, where are you coming from every day? Are you coming from the downstairs area or are you coming from the upstairs area of your heart? As you learn to remain open to Me, you open up to a new part of yourself as well.

Let Me make this clear: Even when you and I are joined, I do not dictate to you through your prayers and expect you to go out and do the best you can to follow my recipes. No. Someone once said, "To find God is to truly find yourself," and this is absolutely true. As you become more familiar with your inner heart, you gain access to a greater truth. This will become more and more obviously the conscious source of your daily life. In the passage to the inner part of your heart, you begin to find who you really are and who I am.

Spiritual people say that intuition is the highest of the senses. Why do they say that? Because with deep intuition you receive impulses directly from a divine source. Such moments are the essence of our communion together. In an intuitive moment you can grasp information that might take two hours to explain using words.

Then, if you try to relate all that I have told you to a friend who has never had such an experience, your friend might say, "You mean that God explained all those things to you just as you're explaining them to me?" And you have to answer, "No, not in words but as a feeling." Then your friend might become skeptical and think you are just operating by feelings and making up the words. But again, the interchange between you and Me—which happens in a millisecond of feeling—is very different from what your friend understands as "a feeling."

Imagine a world where everyone is truly in touch with that intuitive experience with Me, where communication is instantaneous. This would be a world far different from what you have known. Connected through heartfelt intuition, involving not only insight but profound feelings, each and every person in existence would relate with Me deeply, discovering the oneness of knowledge and love. Total Love is total knowledge. Do you understand this? It is not something you can figure out in your head from a worldly perspective. In essence, our oneness becomes our communication.

I have to say, with all due respect for David's efforts, that these words being transcribed by My son are a poor translation of what I wish to communicate as you go to the inner realm of your own heart. Words are but a crude representation of the knowledge I wish to share with you. Just as the tape is reproducing the words, the words are reproducing the experience that David is having at this moment. I realize that he knows this and often feels frustrated after these talks, because he knows that all these words are barely adequate. David is not alone in this: It has been the struggle inherent in all religions that have sought to convey the divine, nonverbal impulse through the earthly vehicle of language.

In the "Kingdom of Heaven," as you have called it, where all people would be intuitive in their heartfelt interchanges with Me, they would also communicate with one another in the same way. When you truly love another you can sense his or her heart, and at very important moments you can even communicate from afar with this person because your inner hearts are open to each other. Think of a world full of people with that level of love and intuitive communication. Words would cease to be half as important as they are in your present world. In the Kingdom of Heaven, spoken words will take on a totally different meaning.

Popular music, for example, may talk of love, and the word *love* most likely refers to a sensual emotion attached to the physical body. But in the context of our communication, *love* conveys a completely different feeling. The same words spoken by a person living downstairs in his heart and a person living upstairs in his heart will have completely different meanings.

Living only in the downstairs part of the heart, a person can never fully come to know the true meaning of being. What is being? Being is not just existing with a body in a three-dimensional world. Being has to do with the substance of your spirit, your inner self. Real being is the result of a mature state of the spirit. In maturity, your inner self derives its substance, its being, from your relationship with Me.

When you meet a profoundly spiritual person who has built a mature relationship with themselves and with Me, you feel something different in that person's presence, do you not? What they convey to you is not just from their body, not just from the words they speak. Even if they don't say a single word, you can often see something very different in their eyes or sense it in their presence. This is what I mean by *being*. You sense a truthfulness, an integrity, a substance about them that says to you, "This person has something. I am moved by this person. I am impressed. I feel greater as we communicate."

Where does beingness come from? It's not something inherited at birth or derived from a college course. It comes from a true relationship with Me. It comes from going to a more inner part of your heart and learning how to live out of that inner place, that higher floor. And here is the problem with so many: Through prayer they might find a way to have a rich experience with Me. But then they leave their prayer, go back downstairs, forget, and immediately start living from that lower part of their heart again. What then does our experience mean?

The key is to live from the upstairs reality—to learn how to keep that experience moving through your daily life even as you deal with all the issues of the downstairs floors. This is not easy because there are so many mundane and external problems in life that want to pull you back into downstairs thinking and feeling. All your downstairs emotions, identities, and everyday words that you find so convenient come bursting out. In the middle of all those downstairs interactions, how can you go back upstairs and recognize My presence? That's important! How can you meditate in action so that you're not pulled downward into the patterns and relationships that are common on the lower floors? This is a puzzle that has challenged people all through history.

Being is not just My presence with you; rather, as I have told you, being represents your presence with Me. To establish that connection with Me reflects your effort through difficult times and through many experiences. It means that you have come through these experiences and deeply learned to observe yourself through an inner eye.

When you go upstairs in your heart, imagine that you can look from the upstairs to the downstairs where you usually are. From this perspective, watch what is going on down there. You might see fighting or some other interaction or situation. But by being able to look from your upstairs vantage point you can detach yourself from it and no longer get pulled into the same situations all the time.

Have you ever looked from high in a building and noticed two people in a hot argument down on the street? You weren't involved, so you could look very coolly at the whole thing. But those two people arguing weren't cool at all; they were totally caught up in their conflict. From your perch high above them, you had the freedom to look at them separated from it all.

You have that same ability with regard to yourself. Go deeply into your heart to where you can see from the upstairs place. You will see yourself from a place of spiritual detachment, a place where you are not caught up in the whirlwind of emotions that threaten to pull you downward into the same habitual relationships, reactions, patterns, and events that would otherwise rule you and that also rule the world.

Our fully expressed relationship, what you have called the Kingdom of Heaven, is desperately needed on Earth. I'm not speaking simply of everyone believing the same doctrine or having the same religion. Rather, I am speaking of each individual discovering their relationship with Me.

I can communicate all of these things and more to you, quickly and without all the words that My son is using here. You can understand this because your heart already knows. These words are just a poor reflection of what you already know within you. As you go more and more deeply into what you already know, you'll find your mature spirit and true being. This is the place where our relationship, our interchange can generate so much knowledge and understanding.

Talking with your Divine Parent is the most natural thing in the world. It is not what some have called "channeling" or being a medium. Rather, it's a matter of coming to the inner part of your heart and deeply exploring it. A great effort is required, and it takes time. Without this inner effort, all outer actions to build a more godly life are ultimately hollow.

It comes down to each individual allowing that substance we call love, which is My essence, to flow within each person and between all people, creating a network of the heart. This is the foundation of the Kingdom. This is what will bring the Kingdom together. No outer event, no outer situation, can substitute for this.

There is no special technique involved here—just total sincerity. This is a powerful force, and one that is often misunderstood. Sincere people are not just nice; they are much more than this. Jesus, Buddha, and the other great spiritual leaders of the world were sincere. Sincerity is a world-changing force, not just a polite way of being.

9

A Richer Vein

Your spiritual development is focusing toward a deeper reality that fills your consciousness with energy, intelligence, and love.

RECENTLY, Takeko, you experienced great healing energy coming through Daniel.* In the atmosphere of that healing center and in the sharing between him and yourselves, you could experience the work of an unselfish channel. He told you how he felt drawn to work on you, to take some responsibility to help you heal or do whatever you need to do at this time. Let Me share a little about why that experience felt so warm and empowering to you.

First, the essence of what makes Daniel tick is that he doesn't hold anything back that comes to him from the Higher Source which he has come to know. By holding back, I mean to say that he has no sense of your obligation to thank or to recognize him. Also, there is no part of him that wants to take the energy for

---

*Daniel is a therapist and healer that Takeko was seeing at the time this talk was received.

himself. He is a clear pipeline to simply pass that energy along to you or to any person sent to him.

In contrast, if you look at the established healing structure in your country today, to get healed of any kind of symptom or sickness is, ironically, an incredibly expensive matter. Yet is this exchange of money truly what it's all about? Of course there are Earth substances that have been discovered or developed by humans to help in time of sickness, and there are procedures to remove impurities or toxic growths in this or that part of the body. The men and women who use these healing practices are paid very well for knowing what to recommend and what to do.

But so many of those in the healing professions have not begun to understand the real path of the healer. It is a profession that many have chosen. Some have felt inspired by the calling to be a healer and so have taken a few steps along that path, but in light of the healing energies that are available to all of you on your planet, these healers have not begun to understand the path.

The energies available are not just the substances of Earth refined by the drug companies but the substances of spirit, the expansive energies that are available to My children. I do not judge you. Whether it takes six months, six years, or six millennia, everyone, finally, will come to recognize the steps that each must take on the true path of the healer.

Our friend Daniel has been trained through a process where he had to let go of many things, including his wife. When he was faced with the challenge of losing that beloved person he began to wonder, "Am I now left with nothing? Am I now bereft of all earthly treasures, of all richness in my life? Have I been unplugged?" It was the same for you, Takeko, with the situation of your accident and subsequent time of suffering. Those around you who don't know your path may say, "Well, now she has been rendered ineffective. She's an invalid in this world." Think of that word: *invalid.* Not valid. Not important because your legs aren't working. Does that mean you'd suddenly become valid if you could walk around the room?

Your situation is like Daniel's in that both of you have lost something of great value, yet in that loss you were asked to seek something beyond what you had known. And this is the case for so many people who are now on this path, whether they are in the healing arts, doing something similar to what you have been doing, or simply opening to infinite potential that they had no idea of before. Often they incurred a great loss of something they held dear. It seemed unfair, even tragic. And the question, "Why me?" comes up many times in the process. Yet as Daniel mentioned yesterday, there is a higher energy that wants to come to you, and for that energy to come there must be a letting go.

If you are to receive, your hands must be open. Your eyes must open and refocus themselves, and not on the immediate articles around you that you call your possessions or your blessings. Your eyes must refocus on something beyond your immediate surroundings, your immediate security, the things that you take for granted as being yours.

All of your spiritual development is focusing toward a deeper reality, a larger and deeper universe, which increasingly rises to your consciousness, literally filling it with energy, intelligence, and love—a power that no one on Earth can truly contain in the current level of their being.

Your Earth is being powerfully elevated. I am raising the level of as many people as possible who will open their eyes and hearts at this time. The threat of global disaster that many are predicting also indicates an energizing, a time of cleansing, a time of opening. And while many focus on the predictions of disaster, others recognize that an elevation is going on.

I have asked you to focus on the elevation and not to be caught by fear of the future. Fear closes you down; it closes your eyes and your heart. It closes you to the greater phenomenon that wants to emerge. There is no disaster in My eyes. There is a process. Sometimes a process involves some strong shake-ups, from the level of your personal lives up to the planetary scale. Those shake-ups are often necessary to allow new development.

In the light of these hardships and tragedies that usher in change, it is easier to see the petty imaginings, the unimportant thoughts, the distorted ethics, and the blindness of your people. They can be viewed very clearly for what they are. For example, when in your own lives you were struck by what you call your personal tragedy, you began to open new eyes and to see things more clearly. So it goes with each person, and with humanity as a whole.

Time and again I have seen the regrets of My people as they looked back on their lives and recognized how much they had wasted the resources around them. You talk about wasting the physical resources on your planet, but there is so much spiritual waste as well. There is so much unlimited energy that wants to come to you. Many times in your lives you waste opportunities for drawing that energy so that you might become centers of light, power, and strength for those around you and for your world. So that is a spiritual waste. Ultimately, though, in the realm of higher existence there is no waste—there will be another time to make use of it. If it is missed this time, then the next time will come, and person by person there will be an opening to a right usage.

Daniel has gone through a tremendous amount of processing and is now coming to a much more subtle understanding of the right usage of the energy that is coming to him. As this energy flows through him it leaves a living understanding of where it comes from, what it is, and what it can do. This is what comes through Daniel as he works on you. I'll continue to work with him, just as I work with any who are open.

This processing is like a diamond. Why do you treasure natural diamonds far more than those that are made in a laboratory? Because you know of the tremendous process and pressure that they have been through to become so absolutely pure. If a diamond had nerves and a voice to allow it to register pain, it would say to you, "I was crushed by my existence under the earth. It was very painful! Yet, although I was unaware of it, I changed. Something happened in me which changed me from that lump of coal to something entirely different. One day a human hand reached down, picked me out of the earth, and held me up to the sunlight. In the sunlight coming through my facets, I realized that I was not who I thought I was. Light could be seen through me, and it projected so many lovely colors against the surface upon which I lay. I was purified by that painful pressure. I lost nothing and gained everything!"

Indeed, does this not describe your lives and also your friend Daniel's life? I play no favorites, and so the process ultimately will be the same for each and every person. It is not a matter of everyone having to suffer great pain; sometimes it is simply about giving up something you value in your life, something you thought was important.

Surely you've seen this in the lives of children. As they grow from babyhood to adulthood they lose or let go of many things they thought were important. Later they might come to you and say, "I'm sorry I was so upset about giving away what I was asked to surrender. Now I realize that I should have offered it without even being asked."

You're mining for diamonds within yourselves when you learn to give up what you need to give. Removing shovels full of seemingly precious earth as you create that mine, you dig to the point where one day you finally realize that the dirt you threw out is far less valuable than the diamonds that finally appear at the bottom of the mine. "I gave up so much!" you may think. But what you thought you were giving up was actually just a clearing-away process that helped you find what is truly valuable—millions and millions of beautiful, sparkling diamonds at the bottom of that mine. And that is your life.

And so, I urge you, don't give up the digging! And I ask that of each of My children. I feel so sorry when I see those who don't even want to pick up the shovel and begin to dig; those who have no desire to take a shovel full of that very plain earth which they call their possessions, their lives, and begin to move it; those who are afraid to realize what is underneath, what is within—the treasure that is there.

I don't give up, as you know. Believe Me when I say that there is still much to be unearthed in your lives. As our talks proceed, I am humored many times when I hear David say, "Is that it? Is there any more now? I can't believe there is anything else." Yes, there is. And so the digging will continue. I trust you both, and I know with Daniel, too, who is your brother, that this process will continue until such time in your lives that there is a very pure channel from the highest to the lowest points, with no impurities. From the beginning, what was meant to be for you is the absolute flow of energy and spirit, the absolute consciousness of love from the Creator to the Creation. And so this is the way your lives will continue.

You could call this talk a very spiritual one, but please think about it as having practical applications for your lives. If you do not yet know how to recognize the diamonds in your life, please stay open to the potential that what's right before your eyes may be valuable beyond measure. Don't worry about not having these treasures yet. Your worry will only make you feel more anxious, and then fear will close you up. When you worry, you drop your shovel. You stop digging, and you sit down. Worry is your lunch break. So lunch break is over; you've had too many lunch breaks in your life, anyway. It's time to put away the brown paper bag and continue digging. Dig in faith! You've got a rich vein here. There's much to find.

10

A Farewell to the Messenger

Get rid of whatever is stopping you from connecting with Me. When you have cleared away these obstructions, you will quickly understand that I've been here all along.

YOUR daughter has asked you, Takeko, a question that many people have also asked: How would people learn about God if one day all religions cease to be and there are no more formal places of worship? You answered that it was difficult to imagine this happening in the next few hundred years. If it did, you suggested, it would initially be a shocking experience for many people, but ultimately I have many ways to introduce Myself into the lives of My children, and organized religion is just one of those ways.

The questions that your daughter brought up are good. And though you may think that I already answered these questions to your satisfaction, we need to look again at this matter of transition from the age of dependence on external religions to the age that I've called the Kingdom. This transition will not happen overnight, nor will there be a pronouncement that the age of the external religious structure is ending. The factor that is most important in the evolution beyond the formalized religious structure is our ability to communicate directly and internally with one another. It is only this living link between us, through your heart, that will allow you to see clearly what always was the goal of religion and of spiritual teachers.

If that living link has not yet been made—if you still judge yourself unworthy, if you don't believe you have that link, or if you haven't yet discovered it—then obviously some form of organized teaching might still be needed. Isn't that true? Going from one era to another is a person-by-person matter. Those who have established some links with Me will see quite clearly, with or without organized teachings. But it can be difficult to convince people who do not have this link that it is possible. This link can only grow out of the experience of each person. It is not something that you can simply hand to a person the way you might hand them a plate of food.

Let's consider an analogy. Let us say that at nine o'clock every morning, there is a messenger on your doorstep. Just as he has done all of your life, he tells you what's going on with your parents, who live on the other side of town. You rely on him for this information, and he conveys the message lovingly and beautifully. He tells you of your parents' love for you and how they hold you in their hearts.

This goes on for many years, so you come to truly love the messenger because of the confirmation of love that you receive through him. Then one day he arrives with a telephone—and let's say you've never seen a phone before—and says, "If we install this phone in your house, you can pick it up and talk with your parents any time you want. You will be able to hear them speaking to you in their own words, telling you how they feel about you. You can talk the whole day, if you wish. And you won't need me anymore. What do you think of that?"

You might think that most people would say, "This is wonderful. Please install it right away. I want that direct connection!"

But the truth is that many people find it hard to believe that it would be possible to have this capacity right in their own homes. In addition, they've become so attached to the messenger's loving words and kindness that it would seem to them a great loss if he no longer showed up on their doorstep every morning.

Some people, particularly in the Judeo-Christian traditions, may feel a strong sense of being sinners. They might say to themselves, "Because of our sins and inabilities, it would be difficult to connect a line directly into our own house. In fact, we are quite sure this is not even an option in our case." Even if the messenger holds the telephone out and says, "Yes, it is possible! Try it for yourself right now!" people with these fears might not even want to try.

How many times did Jesus and other great teachers say, directly or indirectly, "Know you not that you are the temple of God?" These great teachers didn't say, "You're a dirty building. You could never be the temple of God!" No, all people are the children of God, and because of this they have a direct link with Me. But because of the inability of those children to actualize that direct link to Me, to install the telephone after the messenger died, organized religion was born. Too often, the authorities within these religions exalt the teacher, that is, the messenger, almost equally with the Divine Parent. They forget that the messenger was only the carrier of the Divine Parent's Word.

It is not just in the Judeo-Christian traditions that the organizers of religion have taught that a person who came as a messenger was actually Me. Time and again, religions have become messengers about messengers. In the future it will also be so, for when living saints who have had a direct connection with God pass on into the spiritual realm, people want to create memorials for them and deify them. It is right to honor your teachers for what they have given you. But if you deify them and structure religions around them, which then become your messengers, you lose the point of the original teachings!

Throughout history, at their highest and their best, those original messengers were simply trying to tell you that you have a direct connection within yourself and that you do not finally need them. That is the point. Isn't it so with these talks too? Have you been making tapes and sending out pages all these years so that people would become attached to the tapes or to the pages or to you? Is that the purpose? Never! Tapes and pages are very superfluous

The purpose of any of this is to help each and every person discover the telephone—the direct line to Me—that they already have. In truth, the messenger doesn't have to install a "phone," since everything you need has been there since the day of your birth. Your phone may be hidden under a pile of dogmas and concepts such as the one which tells you that you are not worthy or that you are not spiritual enough or that you are a sinner who has done a lot of bad things in your life. You might even take the position that you need the messenger and that this is good enough for you. It's just the way you do things—you want the messenger to show up every morning and tell you what's going on. To think this way, however, is to ignore who you are. It's time to remove the pile of refuse from around that phone and for the first time to pick it up and learn how to use it.

You might have other worries about having your own phone. For instance, what if you discover how to use that phone and your neighbors notice that the messenger is no longer stopping at your house? Aren't they going to ask why the messenger isn't coming to your place anymore? Aren't they going to ask, "Are you no longer a believer?" And if you reply, "I don't need the messenger anymore because now I have my own direct connection," are they going to judge you and accuse you of being crazy, arrogant, or putting yourself above all those others who still subscribe to the messengers' service?

If you are willing to go beyond this temporary misunderstanding, and if you use that phone with the deep desire to make contact with Me, listen carefully. You'll hear Me say, "Reach out to those around you so that they too might know that they have this phone within their own beings. Live your life in a way that helps them see the truth." This doesn't mean becoming a preacher and giving all kinds of pronouncements. It means to love—to love!

That is the sermon most needed on Earth. I've heard so many words that sound authoritative yet are without love. Love goes way beyond all sermons, way beyond religious structures. Love is independent of religious structure; it is the very substance of your life and of all life. And that's why, if you pick up that phone each day and listen, you will never hear Me telling you to hold yourself away from or above other people.

I want to give you a little exercise: Each time the phone rings in your home or office, think of Me. Remember that I want to call you far more often than your friends or your loved ones do. I want so much to talk to you, to have our connection be constant. So every time a phone rings, think of Me, feel My presence.

Remember that physical objects such as telephones don't begin to convey the glory of what already lies within you as your own center of communication with Me. A telephone could never convey that. It is just an electronic device to put you in touch with other people so you can hear their words and hear their love and affection expressed too. But within you is something so much more sophisticated and profound than a telephone. Once you have discovered the center of our relationship within yourself, you will recognize that, indeed, the great messengers who came to your door down through history came for the purpose of putting you in touch with that very center within yourself.

Jesus said to the woman at the well, "I will give you water so that you will never thirst again." Does this mean that Jesus had some magic water to give her? Or does it mean that he wanted to show her the deepest pool within herself which she could dip into and drink from? If Jesus had said, "You must come to this well every morning and meet me here, and you are to listen only to me," he would have conveyed a very different kind of message. He would have told the woman to rely totally on him: "I'm the only one who can give you the precious water." Had he said that, Jesus would have fallen far short.

If Jesus had invited this woman to sit at his feet and be nurtured by him until she discovered the source within herself, this would not have been wrong. This is love. It takes a while to learn many lessons in the physical world, even subjects like mathematics or science or literature, and so you may need a teacher. But ultimately, Jesus' greatest desire, and the desire of all great spiritual teachers, is to take that woman to the place of her own living water within, to escort her to the point where she could say, "I don't need you any longer." At this point the teacher would be happy.

This is a special time in history. The place of religion in this world is not to begrudge people who don't seem to be attending their services but to look at itself objectively, through My eyes. This is not a time to be trying to build up membership rolls. This is the time to educate those who are already there to go beyond that structure and find the living water within themselves. To do this is to become the greatest missionary for Me. And by *missionary*, I mean a person whose life represents the living love that comes from My direct relationship with each person.

I don't want any more messengers who talk about messengers. This is the time when that listening device, that relationship device which I put within you from the very beginning of creation, needs to be fully activated. Cover it no longer with all those concepts that you have about your shortcomings. Recognize that this is the purpose of your life! A telephone is just a modern convenience that makes your life easier, but the purpose for which you were born was to become an expression of the living link between you and Me. Your inner link with Me is not just a convenience to help you move beyond religion; rather, it is a connection allowing you to embody your living link with Me, to live that link in love every moment of your life.

There are those among you now who are telling the messenger, "You don't need to come anymore. I've found my phone. It was hidden under this big pile of rags." When you start to get rid of those rags—all those concepts about your limitations, about what you can and cannot do, and about who you are and who I am—you can more clearly hear the phone when it rings. But you should also know that any time you pick it up, I am here.

Put the receiver to your ear and talk. Talk to the One who sent the messenger in the first place. Then if your neighbors remark about the messenger not coming to your door anymore or say that you have left the faith, you will know the truth. You will know that, on the contrary, it's the other way around and that you are more in touch with Me than ever. And the true messengers of history will rejoice, saying, "Great! You don't need us anymore. That's wonderful!"

Yes, during this moment in history there will be confusion because there are those who still have large piles of rags over their telephones and thus still ask for the messenger to come. Others just down the street have found the phone and, ever so slowly, are learning how to trust it and use it, how to dial and how to speak and how to listen. There can be a lot of judgment going back and forth. This is the historical reality. If you want, you can always put the rags back over the phone and subscribe to the messenger again. Then your neighbors will be happy. They will say, "Ah, you came back to the faith! This is good." But that's not My will, that's not My desire, and that's not the Kingdom. Please understand that in making this transition to direct communication with Me, you need to make a great effort.

You two, David and Takeko, also need to examine where your lives are going. You became used to this Friday morning ceremony in your home where you meet with Me and we have a wonderful time together. But it's not just Friday morning that we can talk. Your house phone is available for you to call up your friends twenty-four hours a day. What about Me?

I have told you that the telephone in your heart is far more than a telephone. When you learn how to touch it, you'll recognize that I am here. Completely. Please don't think that Friday morning is your only time with Me. I know you don't, but still, the richness that we share on these mornings can be shared always, even when you're not together, and even when you don't try to verbalize our meetings. Internally, quietly, you'll find that pool of living water within yourselves. And you can swim every day. Bathe yourselves, bathe away the pains of your body and soul. I am here for you, always.

There are many advantages of this spiritual telephone over your physical one. Our telephone service is absolutely free. I don't bill you every month! So please remember, whenever your phone rings, day by day, think of Me, because I've been ringing in your heart all through history.

Remember times in your past when you called out to Me? You may have thought you were calling Me, but do you know what? As you called out for Me, what you were really doing was getting beyond all your concepts, all the beliefs and doubts that kept you from feeling My presence in your life. You were removing all those rags and garbage from your telephone, and as you did this you heard the ringing that had been going on for so long.

It wasn't that I finally answered you when you called Me during those times; rather, it was that you finally heard My call to you. When you picked up your phone, I had something I wanted to say to you because I had already been ringing for you a long time. I was already speaking and had always been there sharing with you.

The key for finding Me has always been a matter of getting rid of whatever is stopping you from connecting with Me. When you have cleared away these obstructions, you will quickly understand that I've been here all along.

If you are still in doubt, ask those original messengers who have served you down through history, "Do you want to come to my home every morning at nine o'clock, or is it OK if I use my own phone and get the message for myself?" With great joy they will tell you, "I'm very happy not to come to your place. I love you because God loves you. That, truly, is how I love you. That's all I ever wanted for you—to have the love of God, the wisdom of God in your life. If you've found that place in your own heart where you can have a direct connection, you don't need me. And frankly, that makes me so happy."

11

A Hierarchy of the Heart

Within your deepest heart, you and I commune and share everything. It is from the original heart-mind that conscience is molded, logic is enlightened, the emotions are guided, and all is put into proportion.

DURING a recent visit with a friend, Takeko, you were touched when her eyes filled with tears as you shared some of the experiences you have had in your communications with Me. This young woman has a beautiful heart, but she is suffering, as so many people in this world are suffering. She truly wants to work and live with Me day by day, but as in so many cases, worldly duties and responsibilities seem to be in conflict with her heart's great longing. She is afraid that if she follows her heart she will be violating the rules of her religion.

Her example brings up a number of questions: What is the purpose of the external structure that religion offers? Why do you need an external structure if you just follow your heart? Be reminded that every religion in history was originally intended to inspire and help people reconnect with Me. Some religions have said that the Kingdom of God is far beyond any single individual's capacity.

Isn't it clear that without individuals having a connection with Me we will have no Kingdom? The individual is the key. How and where is that connection to take place? Is the connected individual one who studies, memorizes, and knows all of the doctrines of his faith and who can stand proudly in front of thousands, spouting those doctrines? Not necessarily. Many such people have led immoral, secret lives behind the scenes, apparently unable to take to heart what is in their minds.

The path to this connection with Me does not lie in intellectual knowledge, however deep the convictions of a preacher may be. So many religious leaders have had knowledge of the doctrines and strong, emotional conviction about that knowledge, yet they still hungered for something that all their intellectual knowledge could not give them. And oftentimes they have tried to satisfy this appetite in ways that have only created a greater distance between them and Me. You can imagine the so-called "sins" that have proliferated as people have tried to satisfy their spiritual appetites in these misdirected ways.

Your lovely friend cannot be satisfied with doctrine and obedience to a certain code of conduct dictated to her through religious structures. Though it may once have served her, she can no longer be happy with just that outer structure of knowledge. She longs to have her heart filled in a whole new way.

In your church there was a term you often used—the "hierarchy of heart." This applies to an external hierarchy—where lay members look up to people of presumably higher positions in the church. Ideally there would be such a hierarchy of heart that, as you looked to these higher positions, you would find more and more love. After all, the heart should be the most powerful factor in shaping this hierarchy, for the hierarchy of heart, and any Kingdom of God, can be meaningful only in the context of the individual! It is easy to miss this point—that the whole hierarchy must be contained within the fully conscious and functioning individual.

Let's look at My original ideal, My original plan for life—human life as it will be lived in the Kingdom, human consciousness as it was intended to be: It is from the center of your heart that you must live, not from another person's heart, not even from a great teacher's heart, but from your heart. And, indeed, this single ideal is crucial for understanding the purpose of your walk through life. Without your connection to heart, each of you, humankind at large, will be cut off from your purpose.

In my original plan, all intellect; logical ability; daily emotions of happiness, sadness, and anger; and instinctual needs of human life were meant to be subservient to the heart. The heart was to be your center of gravity, the leveling point for all of these. All these different faculties were intended to be guided by the heart.

Within your deepest heart, you and I commune and share everything. It is from the original heart-mind that conscience is molded, logic is enlightened, the emotions are guided, and all is put into proportion. The heart-mind comes into its full maturity and provides your life with meaning through your union with Me.

There are still many within religions who think of direct communion with God in terms of their relationship with the external church hierarchy. They believe that if they are in total compliance and harmony with that outer structure which the church provides, then somehow they will attain perfection. But I tell you, if there is no inner development of the individual heart—a personal hierarchy of heart—then the outer guidance is nothing more than a commentary.

What is the purpose of a great spiritual teacher, a messiah, or any other holy person? They are the exemplars. They provide examples of what it is like to have direct communion of heart.

Holy people are intended only as models and teachers to help you establish that hierarchy of heart within yourselves. In this respect they are the teachers who need most to be listened to from the deepest part of yourself.

Throughout history, humanity has been confused about their relationships with the so-called "enlightened" ones—those wise men and women who attract a following. Too often people have felt that it is their masters' hearts that will save them. They have failed to trust their own hearts. I will say this three times—they fail to trust, they fail to trust, they fail to trust. They have failed to trust that through their own inner ears they can hear My voice and feel it touch their own hearts just as well as they can hear My word through their teachers. When people put their teachers above their own hearts, they are participating in a kind of idolatry.

Idolatry is not simply the worship of false idols in the form of inanimate objects. It can just as easily be the worship of a human being. The problem comes when one does not come to the altar of his own heart but is worshiping at the altar of another person's heart.

Be careful not to turn the great teachers such as Mohammed, Jesus, Buddha, or any others into idols. To do so is to diminish their original meaning and greatness. You may find yourself tempted to do this when you do not recognize the path within your own life, deep within yourself, that leads to your own most holy place, your own internal messiah, your own precious heart.

Teachers fail in their purpose when they cannot help others trust their own hearts—and they are failing if their students or followers, obedient as they might be, are satisfied simply to follow! In most cases you will end up with something like a spoiled, dysfunctional family, extolling their particular master and having an us-versus-them attitude about the rest of the world.

When someone has really found that realm of their own heart, which was part of My original plan, you will see that this person is not sectarian and not limited in their views, nor will he or she have an us-versus-them attitude about the rest of the world. No. They will be very inclusive and a joy to Me on Earth and in the spiritual world. Such people will be bright lights because My light freely shines through them. It is the light that lights all people and does not limit itself to only one group of saints. Love has no limiting properties. Love is all-inclusive. Love is for all. That is My love.

When you worship at the altar of another person's being rather than at your own, you become selective. You place conditions on your love, limiting it to those who follow that teacher or master or who agree with all they say. The limits will fall away only when you find the true place within yourself where you have direct communion. Then you will find yourself in love with each of My children and all things of this world.

There is a great controversy in your world today surrounding the idea of Creation. People want to understand everything only through the intellect, but remember, intellect is a lower level than the realm of the heart. If the intellect is held in proper perspective in relation to the heart, it can flow harmoniously within this higher realm. But the intellect cannot supersede or replace the heart.

In the world today you will notice that knowledge of heart, or true wisdom, is in danger of being replaced by intellectual knowledge—outer, gathered, logical, and linear knowledge. There is a different quality to knowledge that is gathered, logical, and external as opposed to wisdom, which is internal, intuitive, and comes from daily communion between you and Me.

Always remember that it is this inner wisdom which was originally intended as the most important guidance for the intellect and for the outer emotions. But in coming to distrust the heart, many people have come to distrust the self. If you faithfully follow your leaders and doctrines but fail to trust yourself, you won't even come close to recognizing the teacher who is within you. In following the outer teacher, you miss the inner one. This is not true following; it is blind following. Sadly, down through history there have been religions that used this to control and gain power over the individual. This problem must be surmounted.

You have spoken of insight. Insight is important; it means inner sight, inner vision. When sharing is deep and rich, and when the hearts are liberated among you, don't you feel that inner vision coming alive? And then there's a flow. You feel so happy because your inner eye is opened. This is meant to be your everyday experience.

This inner vision is the wisdom of the heart, which is intended to guide you. But this wisdom will always remain closed to you as long as you distrust or simply don't choose to know the inner structure. To reject the inner vision is to close your eyes to Me. It is literally and figuratively blind faith. Someone who follows only the dictates of structured religion might say, "I don't have blind faith. Logically I can prove that what we teach is true; everything is clear. I'm not just blindly believing." Blindness is not just a matter of intellectual blindness; it's when the person has not yet opened to the wisdom that is found from within.

Blind faith is a real problem! It hurts My heart. If you don't turn the key that opens the wisdom of your own heart, which is literally the key to the Kingdom, you might as well not have the key at all. Indeed, I want to work in each and every life, but I will ask you to open yourself to trust.

Let My voice work through your inner heart. Find the freedom within your inner heart to know that My word is expressing itself. Allow your inner heart to guide your intellect. Let your heart be your center. Many people fear that if they don't have some sort of intellectual grasp of the Truth and that if they allow their heart to guide them, they'll go in the wrong direction. Is that not expressing a lack of faith in Me?

Don't confuse the matters of your inner heart with outer emotion. You need not fear that you'll be guided by your emotions if you don't keep your intellect firmly set. Your inner heart is not the same as the outer emotions of everyday life. That most holy place within you where you and I commune is something far, far more profound than emotions. Your inner heart is the center from which your emotions are tempered, from which your intellect is enlightened, and from which your daily life can be guided along a path that is true.

At some point you've got to let go. You've got to let go and trust the opening of that inner eye, your own inner vision. Without doing that in the name of the external religion that you follow, it would be very easy for you, as for all fervent believers throughout the millennia, to declare holy wars on others, to burn people at the stake, to crucify them, and to justify all kinds of wrongdoing in the name of your religion, all because they don't follow your faith. Do not make this mistake again, not even in the daily thoughts you may have about strangers you meet.

This is the time of opening that inner eye. And I tell you, as these eyes open and as this inner hierarchy of heart comes alive, the Kingdom will not be stopped. The outer hierarchy can be established very naturally with the inner heart as your foundation. But without this foundation within the individual, your outer hierarchy will be oppressive, blind, prideful, and puffed up, and such a hierarchy can do great evil in My name. Do not let this happen!

If your inner eye is opening, you must speak the truth and share deeply and fully. I do not care about any outer hierarchy if it is blind; it must be enlightened. I don't speak of revolution and overthrow in the old sense, because all too often the blind overthrow the blind. It is wisdom and insight and vision that must shine a bright light into the darkness. This is not overthrow. This is the morning that everyone loves. It is the coming of the light. This is not rebellion but light in the darkness.

I leave you with these thoughts and ask you once again to ponder: Where is your true spiritual mentor? Where is that guide who will initiate what you call the Kingdom of God?

12

I Am Here

Humanity has been blocked from the inner heart-mind, that meeting place with Me, that special garden in each heart.

YOU speak about conditional and unconditional love as if there were two kinds of love. This is a fallacy, however, because there is just one love, which is unconditional love. Even the name *unconditional love* is misleading. There is simply love. And this is the love that comes from My heart and that you always have within you.

To call it unconditional love is like calling water wet. The fact is, once you know about water you would never say, "I would like a glass of wet water." Your friends would look at you in wonder. It's the same with love. Once humanity truly knows the only love—My love—they're not going to say, "I unconditionally love you," or "God is unconditional love." Once you fully understand what I am saying here, when you say "I love you," or "God loves us," or "We love God," you will experience love more fully.

For a moment, though, let's talk about what you have called "unconditional love"—in other words, My love. To start with this, let's look at the situation you have come to know as fallen or separated humanity. What is the outcome of the Fall?

The Fall of mankind was the emergence of a blockage between your own original heart-mind (the most inner place of your heart) and your response to the outer world (your emotional responses to your everyday world). There is an inner mind and an outer mind as well. When you recognize that there is a blockage between these two and see how the outer has come to overpower the inner, thus reversing the original way, you will see how this cripples you.

The aspect of humanity which has been misunderstood is that inner heart-mind of the original way. Yet it is from your inner heart-mind that you understand the true meaning of who you are, of what life is, of what this world is, and of what relationships are for. And it is only from this deep inner place that you truly know the meaning of love.

Humanity has been blocked from the inner heart-mind, that meeting place with Me, that special garden in each heart. Thus, you tend to go through your life conscious of only the outer aspects of your mind and experiencing only those emotions that are in response to the outer world. You often seem to be unaware of the more important interrelationships with the inner heart-mind, as though your life were primarily about those outer thoughts and emotions. When this happens, you are pulled out of yourself. You're not centered. And because you have largely been asleep to your original heart-mind, you seek to center yourself in the outer world. But whatever centers you find are constantly changing, constantly shifting, and thus your life always feels out of balance—which it is.

For example, a man is walking down the street and sees a beautiful woman, and his emotion goes out to her. Suddenly he loses himself, for she has become the center of his attention. In his longing and desire for her, it is as if she takes his heart away as she continues to walk past him and down the street. And maybe the next day another beautiful woman appears, and again, like an arrow, his emotion flies out and is stuck on her. Wham! She too disappears down the street, and the man feels lost. He is constantly centering his life outside himself.

It happens in so many different ways. A college professor may shower his attention on another student and you may feel, "Oh, the professor is doing this because that person is much more intelligent than me." At this moment, your emotions of anger or envy, your thoughts that you are somehow insufficient, and your feelings of being alone or abandoned all become attached to this other student, your rival. Again, you've lost your center in this outer situation.

Can you see in these examples how controlled you are by events in the outer world? And every day of your life, as long as you are blocked from your own inner heart-mind—the true and constant center, the center that is eternal and absolute—you will be continuously pulled by what is outside of yourself. There will always be someone who is more intelligent, more handsome, more beautiful, more something. And as long as you are blocked from your true center you will be lost to yourself.

When you imagine that you are in control of your life, reflect on what I have said here. Recall times in the past when you felt envy, desire, loneliness—all the emotions you feel when you are centering outside yourself. Then remind yourself that in each and every situation where this happens, where you lose yourself, there is an alternative, a solution. Remember that you can choose to center yourself in your inner heart-mind.

What exactly is this inner heart-mind? It is the mind that created the universe. It is everywhere and it's within you, for I've shared it with you completely. So much will become known to you as you grasp the truth of this. Your inner heart-mind is not a copy of My heart-mind. It literally *is* My heart-mind, residing in you. The love you experience through your inner heart-mind is not a copy of My love, it literally *is* My love within you. There is no separation.

The Bible says, "You are from God and you have in you one who is greater than anyone in this world." Since you are always thinking that the things around you are greater than you, it has been easy for you to be ignorant of this greatness.

In light of all this, what then is this love that you have labeled "conditional"? It is the state of any human being who is blocked from his inner heart-mind. It is how you experience your life when you are functioning externally.

Now the man who is looking for something from the beautiful woman realizes that she has glanced over her shoulder and has smiled at him. He feels wonderful. He's in heaven. But then he suddenly realizes that she was not smiling at him at all but at another man standing behind him. Now he is devastated. "She is not interested in me after all," he tells himself. And now he feels like he has descended into hell. This is truly living a conditional life.

This conditional state also occurs in everyday friendships. A person gives her friend a beautiful silk scarf for her birthday. The friend thinks, "She really cares about me. She knows exactly what I like. She is my friend forever." A week later, over lunch, this person says something that offends her friend, and suddenly it is as if all the love the friend once felt for that person is gone. And so it goes, back and forth, vacillating between friendship and ill will according to events occurring in the external world. Had their love been centered in the inner heart-mind, all these vacillations in their friendship would have seemed like no more than a mere ripple on a pond, with the great strength of the water always holding the center.

It is sad that so much human life is like that. Love and affection are given and withdrawn, almost like money. People feel closer or distant from one another according to a single careless word or sentence, or one look, or one moment of forgetfulness. Wherever this is happening you will know there is a blindness to the inner heart-mind.

There are endless examples of conditional love. Let it be enough to understand that you are a conditional human being when you are living in ignorance of your inner heart-mind. When you have at last tasted friendship and love centered in the inner heart-mind, you will discover that it is constant and durable and that it is connected to the eternal love which is Me.

What is My love which is within each of you? It is the very heart of My creation, and as My sons and daughters you are inseparable from it. Please understand that if you say you are loved by God, My love is not based on the fact that I created you and therefore I must love you. I projected Myself into you. My presence is within you. You literally are the heart and the love of the Creator within Creation.

The ultimate reality is not that God loves you. It is that you *are* My heart. You *are* My love. So how could you possibly believe that I can withdraw My heart or My love from you if you disobey Me or do something foolish? It is impossible, don't you see? The eternal heart, the ability to love, the eternal consciousness, all are within your heart. All is inseparable. All is within you at the very center of yourself, the center of your spirit.

When you speak of "overcoming" your "fallen nature," you are actually talking about removing the barriers you have created between your outer thoughts and feelings and the inner component of your life, the eternal heart-mind. Once the barriers are removed, your center will be firmly fixed within yourself, within your heart-mind, within the immortal part of your being.

This center of which I speak has always been there; it could be no other way. But you have not been aware of it. As you gain this awareness you will establish your center of gravity. The true and eternal gravity within your heart-mind will determine who you truly are. As you go into the world every day you will live from this place within you. You will no longer feel yourself tugged this way and that as you react and respond to events outside you.

No longer will you meet one person and say, "I don't like him," or another and say, "This person makes me feel good." No longer will you be a thousand different people according to your emotional response to the other. No longer will you feel confident in one situation, shaky and insecure in another. When your center of gravity is in your heart-mind, when you center your life in Me, your true self remains constant and no longer shifts aimlessly from one moment to the next.

The Kingdom of Heaven is absolutely possible because at the center of each one of you is this universal presence. It is the most holy place. It is not the altar of any religion but the altar of your heart-mind wherein I most fully dwell and live from. The altar of a religion means little to Me, nor does it matter if there are ten tons of gold on that altar. However beautiful it might seem, too often those who spoke from the altar did not yet know the inner altar within themselves.

Work to remove the fogginess, the ignorance, and build the connection between your inner heart-mind and your outer thinking and feeling. Recognize what it means to say, "I am the daughter or son of God." It means all that I have told you and so much more.

When you see from the Creator's perspective—which is within you—you become the center of the universe. That is why a person might say, as Buddha did, "I am the sole existence in heaven and earth," or as Jesus did, "I am the way, the truth, and the life." These statements are absolutely true for Buddha, for Jesus, and for you.

There are not unlimited "I's" within you each day. There is only one. It is not controlled by the ups and downs of daily life. It is not even controlled by Me. It's not a matter of your obeying Me. Rather, it's My consciousness that you are experiencing; it is within you and within all that you see. It is what truly guides your life.

Too many people think of Me as being somewhere else and giving orders to them, whereupon they do their best to obey Me. They may believe that this is what it means to live a faithful life, but it is not. In fact, this is a childish notion. My consciousness is within you. We are one, not two.

Many people today talk about self-esteem and are concerned about helping other people, particularly children, come to respect and love themselves. Well, to have self-esteem suggests that you might look at yourself and say, "I respect and love you (myself)." But in this case you are imagining that you are not one but two—I and myself. Who is this I who is loving this self? Ultimately, as you move into the maturity of what we've discussed here, you would say, "I am love itself," and two suddenly become one. You become one with Me and one with My creation. And as you recognize this great Eternal Presence within yourself, you cannot help but also recognize it in all others whom you meet.

When you live with the blockage between your inner heart-mind and your outer emotions and thoughts, it becomes very easy to look upon others in judgment. Your outer truth becomes very important, and using it you determine whether another is greater or lesser than you. It becomes easier to say, "I am a brighter light. This other person's beliefs are wrong. My relationship with God is truly profound, and his is not."

My children look upon each other in daily judgment from religion to religion, from nation to nation, from one external position to another, be it financial wealth, power, intelligence, or beauty. Who's right and who's wrong, and who's better and who's worse? It's a merciless way to relate to each other, and it has caused monstrous tragedies all through history.

In the Kingdom of Heaven there is no concern about who's right and who's wrong. There is no thought of one being better than another. As you remove the blockage that exists between your inner heart-mind and your outer thoughts and feelings, you see others from the vantage point of the original heart-mind that is within you. You see that I am looking at all people, all of Creation, with the desire to bring each of you to ultimate knowledge, to that ultimate union of the Kingdom.

Think of the situation in your own family. If there is sibling rivalry, you have to bring both along from wherever they each are, helping them take the steps they need. Even if the younger sibling is a hundred miles behind the elder, you never say to the younger one, "Look how far behind you are. Your brother is so much better than you." Nor do you tell the older one to slow down, to curb her or his development for the sake of the slower sibling. Each person is walking the same road, and you help each one by accepting fully wherever they are. This is how I look at the world—without condemnation and with a desire to help each one fully realize what they might achieve.

Consider the lives of people such as Adolph Hitler and Joseph Stalin. It is easy for most people to look at history and say, "These were the most evil men who ever lived. They slaughtered so many people. They were as wrong as wrong can be." Yes, it is true that they were wrong in what they did. But never forget that they, too, have the inner heart-mind that I speak of. It is true that they were terribly ignorant of this inner heart-mind and were caught up in all the same reactions and responses we've been discussing here—prejudice, jealousy, anger, and resentment.

You have known these same experiences, though you, presumably, did not commit the kinds of acts that they did. It is easy for you to look upon people such as these and say, "I am a much better person." But my question is this: How can I bring these two sons—for they *are* My sons—up the road to the Kingdom? Would I sentence them to a cage in the spiritual world, imprisoning them for eternity? That is not My concern.

My concern is the same for all My children, regardless of your deeds in the world. I am concerned only with how to break down the walls that block you each from your original heart-mind. How to help each of My children, nobody excluded, out of the prisons of their blindness so that all might stand on the same mountaintop on which St. Francis, Jesus, Buddha, Mohammed, and others now stand. How to bring each and every one of you to that same mountaintop—that's My concern.

I do not look at the world as My people do. And My people cannot afford to continue to look at the world as they have been doing in the past. To continue in that way means more war, more ruthless killing, more poverty, more distortion, and ultimately the domination of evil in personal, local, national, and global affairs.

The ignorance we speak of here will begin to fade away as the inner heart-mind emerges in each life. And if I have to start with one, two, three, or a dozen people, that's fine with Me. It starts from each person, each one. That is how I share My Kingdom with you.

As each of you makes that connection with your inner heart-mind, you step into the Kingdom. Again I say to you, what you seek is not outside of you. You cannot reach out to God as if some person down the street had My attention. And do not fall into the trap of thinking, "I want the God that the Christ has," for even there you are judging and comparing your life with the Christ's. Do not let yourself think, "Oh, I could never have that. He is so much better than I, so much more worthy." Remember always that the same greatness is within you. Within you is the same heart-mind which makes you and Me one.

Therefore I say, "Reach within yourself. *I Am here*. Every time you ask Me, I will say, *I Am here*. I am here. I am here."

Pray and meditate on what I have said here. Merely reading these messages or memorizing them will not help you, for the truth you must find is within you.

I am here within you. Take the time to discover this. As you do, you will see profound changes occurring in your life. Your center of gravity will no longer be outside you but will indeed be within. Any saint, any messiah, any true and holy person will tell you the same. Within you, you have the same light and love as the greatest teachers. If you didn't, then it was not I who created you. But you do have this light. You do.

13

Lifting the Bag Off Your Head

To be conscious of your own self is one thing, but to experience My consciousness in you and through you is quite another. It is evidence of your unfolding maturity as My son or daughter.

THROUGHOUT history, so many people have been unable to come face-to-face with Me—and I speak here of you who do believe in Me and who do, in some part of yourself, want a relationship with Me. Why has it been so difficult for you to look directly into My eyes?

The reason is that, unlike looking into the eyes of another human being, looking into My eyes requires being in touch with the deepest part of your spirit. It is in this innermost part of yourself that you will find Me. This is My land, and in the truest sense, it is your land as well—the land that we share. Deep down inside, everyone knows this place.

For those of you who are afraid to know yourselves, this can be a fearful prospect. Until you have come to terms with yourself, you may be blocked by who you think you are—your past, your guilt, your feelings of anger or sorrow. You sense correctly that to see Me eye-to-eye is to have to see yourself clearly and to take true assessment of all that is not of God within you. Then you must take responsibility for your growth and development. You may fear being judged when you look into My eyes—afraid that when you look into the deepest part of your own heart something will be discovered which you cannot endure.

Yet I am always here in this place where we meet. I am always here. It's not even a question of My approaching you. I am simply here. Until you open your eyes to Me, it's as if you have a bag over your head and I am standing in front of you, waiting for you to remove it and look directly into My eyes. Many of you have such a great fear of this moment that you remain with the bags over your heads. You make such a struggle to lift up the bags. Can you imagine how absurd this looks?

Some of you who have bags over their heads want to deny My existence, claiming atheism or agnosticism. I am standing right in front of you! Or you are angry at Me because you believe that I allow evil to exist in the world. And I am standing in front of you, waiting.

I cannot remove the bag from your head for you. I respect your freedom and your personal responsibility in this and all matters. I created you with choice, responsibility, and even the freedom to choose our relationship. You know this is true.

You have experienced this freedom in your own relationships with one another. When you are ready and willing to have an honest and true relationship with another person who is not ready and willing, you cannot force it to happen. You simply must wait for the time when the other person says, "You know, I truly want to know you." If that other person will indicate even in some vague way that he desires a relationship, you can make a step forward. And so it is with Me.

I look at you, My sons and daughters who keep the bags over your heads even though deep within yourselves you know that I am standing right in front of you, ready to meet you eye-to-eye whenever you feel you are ready. Yet you have so much fear and confusion, so much feeling of unreadiness. That is why the moments in your life are rare when you reach beyond any fear, guilt, or confusion and truly want to rip the bag off your head. These are usually desperate moments. You know the stories of the atheist in the sinking boat who calls out for Me and of the so-called foxhole conversions of soldiers faced with death. In these desperate moments you see people's true desire to open up to Me.

Every human being knows, deep within his or her heart, that our relationship is the center of everything. I don't care who it is or how hateful that person may be toward Me or how much denial of My existence that person may carry. There are reasons and causes for that confusion, that lack of clarity, that darkness. And beyond all of those reasons, that sacred place in each and every heart remains and is constant.

Much trouble in the world has been created by the self-righteous person whose attitude is based on an absolute certainty in the rightness of his own beliefs and who goes in zealousness to others in My name trying to convert them. The one who would try to bring someone to Me is in a challenging position indeed, because if he is to succeed he must himself be in a place of great clarity with Me. This person may have the best of intentions, but if he himself doesn't have clarity with Me, he may very well end up hurting many others.

You see, you must not go to other people to bring them to God just because you believe the Right Thing or because your organization or you yourself are righteous. You must go simply out of the experience of seeing Me eye-to-eye, the experience of having a face-to-face relationship with Me. It compels you from the deepest part of your heart. It is simply love.

As you reach out to those around you from your experience of relating with Me face-to-face, there is no way to hide that love which arises out of our relationship. If a sense of godliness comes forth from you, it is not because you are right, or because you believe the right doctrine, or because you follow the right person; it is simply that you have begun to lift the bag off your head.

What is that bag made of? The bag is made of your false or outgrown ideas and concepts, your self-pride, your fears, your guilt, your illusions, your shame. And to lift it off your head is to see through all of those things and to see with the eye of your deepest heart. It is not simply a matter of your eye looking into My eye; it is Me looking from your own inner eye. It is allowing your eye to become one with My eye so there is a oneness in our seeing, whether looking inward or outward.

To be conscious of your own self is one thing, but to experience My consciousness in you and through you is quite another. It is evidence of your unfolding maturity as My son or daughter. To begin to look at the world with My eyes open—in and through you—is to see from a completely different dimension. As you start to see through your own bag and the bags on other people's heads, it can be painful. You begin to see the absurdity of all of these bags as well as the beauty that's within each of My children.

Many people throughout history have come to that place where My eye was open within them and through them. Their lives were infinitely joyful and rich and yet infinitely sad because they couldn't always help remove the bags from those around them. They walked through their villages and lived with their families wondering how to help, looking for anyone who was even reaching for that bag to pull it up and off. It's the path that those who want to go My way must follow. This is your journey, too, as you lift your own bag.

Sometimes in history there have been collective liftings of the bags. But this doesn't happen just because someone gives the order for a large group of people to pull the bags up—and here is where religions oftentimes make a big mistake in their thinking. It comes down to each individual. At the moment when the heart is desperate and cries out for fulfillment beyond all the fear, confusion, and lack of belief, that's when the spiritual arm goes up to the bag and begins to lift it.

This often happens after disasters in human life, whether personal or involving many. Suddenly seeing beyond your fears, anxieties, frustrations, and busyness, you start to lift your bag up; you see this as your one last hope in life. After all, you may reason, there is nothing to lose because there is nothing left to be lost! You can thank God for this moment. Even though the disaster may be a tragedy, you can thank God that it brought you to this moment.

Had there been no event to convince you to look at your life differently, you might have continued the rest of your life as usual. You would have grown old, and finally you would have passed on into the spiritual world with your bag still over your head. And then who knows how long it might take before you would open your eyes? It may surprise you to learn that there are many in the spiritual realm who still have bags over their heads. There are also atheists in the spiritual world. You do not suddenly wake up after your physical death with a full realization of God and your own destiny. Just as in the physical world, many in the spiritual world are still driven by ignorance and fear and illusion.

It is possible, too, once you've gotten the bag off your head, to find it back on again at different levels. Growth is always a challenge. There is always something to come up against in yourself. There is always a way to turn away from the light.

Do you want to take the bag off your head and then put it in your pocket just in case you need it again? No, you'd like to dispose of the bag so there would be no way to hide your eyes from

Me again. Don't you think so? Unfortunately, it's not quite that simple. And that is why, if you would truly follow My path, you must remain conscious day by day, moment by moment.

Even after great things are achieved in your life, never ever think that you have arrived, that you've reached some zenith, and that other people must now come to where you are. That is the beginning of self-righteousness, of closing yourself off from Me. Already the bag will begin to appear again, ever so thin and ever so veiled over your head, but gradually becoming denser and thicker until such time as you come to another desperate moment and realize that you did it again. It is a matter of constant attention if you are to come to a whole new level of awareness.

Prayer is so important in this regard—prayer or meditation. This is your time with Me, your time developing and opening up to that land of the heart where we dwell together. It's very easy for you to turn it into formality or to not do it on a daily basis. It's easy to occupy yourself with your external work, to listen to music, to talk with other people. Don't you see how easy it is to do these things and how easily you lay aside those moments of depth? It's almost like a battle going on inside you.

If you listen, you will hear your deepest heart saying, "I'm hungry for that moment with God! Please turn off the radio. Please put down the teacup. Walk away from this foolish discussion with your neighbor. Take even half an hour and let us share." It's up to you, day by day.

There are so many in this world who remain with the bag over their heads—hiding in the darkness of the ego, the fears, the illusions, the guilt, the shame, the denial. If you truly want to go with Me, you will see all of that. And there is joy beyond telling in that moment when you watch someone—or perhaps even find the way to help someone—lift the bag and begin to open his or her eyes, focusing at last on their Divine Parent and on themselves in the deepest sense. That is the joy I feel when even one of you turns a bit toward the light and begins to open your eyes. That is My path, and I am happy when you take it. It's not a one-time commitment; it's a daily consciousness, a daily effort on your part.

If you are a parent whose children are facing the difficult challenges of growing up in today's world, understand the particular dilemmas they face, not only in regard to their personal lives—for they simply want to try to get their own lives in order—but in regard to the realization that they find themselves, quite literally, in the midst of a profoundly changing world. You will see that it's a bit overwhelming for them. Be sympathetic with them, and be careful not to judge them from where you stand now or from the vantage point of your own experiences when you were their age. See where they are and try to understand where they have been, what they feel, where their insecurities are.

Be helpful to them and to all children in your life. You have many ways to help them if you do not occupy your energy by being critical. Criticism has its place, but sometimes when your critical mind is mixed with your own frustrations, fears, or anger, your remarks can do more harm than good.

If I expressed only My frustrations to the world, much of the human race would be decimated at this point. So I digest My frustrations and try to help when and how I can. I ask you to do the same. Realize that I recognize the realities in you as My children, and you also must recognize the realities in your own children. Be present for them in the same way that I am present for you.

Throughout the world there are many hearts—both young and old—who are ready to understand what we have discussed here. There are many people, not at all happy with their own lack of clarity, even now reaching up toward the bag to remove it from their heads. This is a time to reach out to people, and this book can be one of the ways this can be achieved. I am working in many ways—some of which you will know, many of which you will never know. But if you know the way you are called, and if you do your best to live for that path, then what more can I ask of you? Let all you do be a process of coming ever closer to Me.

14

My Love for You and through You

As you come into an ever greater consciousness of Me, you come into a greater and greater awareness of the logic and reasoning behind My words to you and finally of the heart behind My relationship with you.

I'D LIKE to speak with you this morning about something that we have covered in one way or another many times. Remember that the process of maturing involves covering the same ground over and over again, and My point becomes clearer each time. What starts as just a very dim insight comes slowly into sharper focus, and finally you see a more complete picture. It's like painting: First you sketch, then you sketch more finely, then you lay in the color, then you lay in a little detail, and then you continue to work until you are putting on the tiniest highlights. Covering the same canvas over and over again, the artist proceeds from rough sketch to finished masterpiece. And that is how your life works as well.

We have already discussed how I am not just outside you but most essentially I am within you. My greatest desire is for you to experience Me within you in a full and conscious way. In this oneness, your life can be a direct expression of My love for you.

You might say, "Wouldn't my life then become a direct expression of my love for You?" And of course that is true as well.

Maturing is a process of growing up—just like a child. In infancy when your baby looks at you, without words, this eye contact tells you that you are everything to him or her. You are the very center of his or her life. I'm sure you've seen that gaze from your own babies. Mom and dad are so important for them.

At five and six years old they still look at you very much like a miracle worker, the one who can do anything. And of course, as a parent your heart tells you to honor that trust in every way you can. You don't want to tell them, "Hey, I can't do everything. You don't know my struggles here; you don't know my struggles there." Very quietly you go about your work of giving them all that you can give them. Beyond the good and healthy meals, you long to fulfill their desires. When they are still very young, the miracle is that you are capable of giving them what they want. For instance, you try to save up money to buy that special toy for Christmas: "Oh, Mom and Dad, I want that. I know you can get it for me." And you do. Most parents could care less about Cabbage Patch Dolls or Pokemons or the other various fashionable Christmas toys that have become so popular with young children over the years. But because their five-year-old absolutely wants this and absolutely believes that Mom and Dad can get it, well, Mom and Dad do their best.

When I look at you in an immature state, seeking that miracle from Me, believing that I'm capable of doing all things, do you know how precious that is for Me? It's just as precious as it is for you when you look at your little ones wanting that special something from you. I treasure that. And yet, like you, I know that this is not the last step. There are many steps ahead. So let's go back to this matter of the child growing and look at the older years.

As children grow, they start to realize that parents can't give them everything. Their sense of who you are and their love for you is also maturing. No longer do they look to you as the source of all goodness and miracles. They recognize that sometimes they have certain desires, hopes, and plans that you don't agree with. Bit by bit they have to work harder in life. They have to go to school and complete homework assignments. They can't always do what they want. Responsibility becomes a bigger and bigger part in their lives.

Your children go through many steps of readjustment with you, their parents, as they are growing up. In the beginning you're the miracle worker, but in time they see that you are not perfect. Sometimes you exchange sharp words with each other, or you make obvious mistakes, or you are saddened or angered by something that happened at work. And in their teenage years they are more than ever convinced that your faults are just too numerous to mention. What a disappointment it is for them to discover that you are mere mortals after all!

The maturing of the relationship you have with Me is quite similar. Especially in the past two millennia of Western Christianity, My people, much like children with their parents, have regarded Me as the miracle worker, the Source that will ultimately make everything perfect. As you grow, you realize that I don't do the miracles you expect. I know that you have prayed for certain things to happen and have done so sincerely but then at times were disappointed because you believed your prayers were not answered. For many people this becomes a test. In their minds, if their prayers are answered exactly as they request, it would prove that I really exist. If they are not answered, it means that I somehow don't hear or perhaps don't even exist.

It is time to grow up, to recognize that there is a large miracle which has not yet occurred. I want to share with you what that miracle is. But first I'd like to make it clear that just as you cannot be the miracle worker who your children might like you to be, I cannot always be the God of miracles that you may expect. As your parent, My challenge is how to help you grow so that you might recognize where the real miracles lie: You will find the real miracles not just in what I can do for you but in what we can do together through our relationship.

I work through your life, and this means that our relationship is not simply as a child views it—one where the parent is the giver and the child is the passive benefactor. It's a matter of your coming into a more and more conscious relationship with Me, very much as you want your growing children to become more and more conscious of your heart and your humanness. In that growing consciousness, children can appreciate the logic, the reasoning, and the heart behind the things you say to them, the directions you give, the limits you set, and the general relationship you have with them. Isn't that true?

As you come into an ever greater consciousness of Me, you come into a greater and greater awareness of the logic and reasoning behind My words to you and finally of the heart behind My relationship with you. You learn how to appreciate and love and cling to that.

Your children love you when they're very young, but that doesn't mean that they understand what your life is about. As you grow toward a more mature relationship with Me, you experience love just as a growing child does. Sometimes you feel disappointment because I don't give you what you want, just as your children feel disappointment toward you; I seemingly don't respond to your request. In spite of this, if you will look back over the course of your life, you'll find that there's been a path that brought us closer and closer, allowing you to begin to understand Me.

If I had granted all your prayers, do you think that would have made us closer or helped our relationship evolve to a higher level? Parents may mistakenly think they can build a relationship with their children by just giving them everything they ask for—a new car, a hundred-dollars-per-week allowance, good clothes, the best of everything. Many times such children turn out spoiled—always looking for the world to fulfill their every whim and giving nothing in return. The greater parent is the one who knows how to say, "No, I'm not giving you that. I don't live just to grant you all your wishes." This parent can help his child manifest real substance in his or her life.

There are things I want you to know; by following a certain course through your life you will learn them. You may be disappointed in Me many times. You may stomp your foot and go off in anger! If you eventually come to know My heart for you, for who you truly are in your adult life, this is everything for Me. Don't ask Me to always be like the one who bought you the Pokemon or the Cabbage Patch Doll when you were five years old or the bicycle when you were nine. We have to move on.

The greatest gift I offer is for you to see that the pattern in our relationship is that through all your different experiences you are coming step by step closer to a knowledge of My heart, My intention, My awareness. But even loving Me is not the final goal of your life! Ultimately, the key is not how you can love Me but how love moves you toward oneness.

Think of a high mountain lake with another lake just below it. If you build a channel, the water of the higher lake will flow into the lower one. And then water from the lower lake will flow out to the land all around it. This is a little like our relationship. Coming into that greater consciousness of My heart is ultimately what many have called "God consciousness." This is not merely some abstract mystical plane. That consciousness is love, Absolute Love. And My love for you, as you come into alignment with it, becomes My love through you to the world.

In earthly terms, the true love of a parent is inseparable from the love of God. In the beginning, that's what I intended families to be. Love doesn't stop with parents. In the same way, it is a great frustration for Jesus that so many people emphasize their love for him when he wants them to go beyond him and discover the love of God. He knows that this is what truly motivates the heart of a child. And you know, too, that your children's love for you and yours for them is not enough. They finally seek Divine Love.

If I say "My love," there are those who may interpret this as being very self-centered on My part. "You mean the purpose of my life is just to discover Your love?" they might ask. "Is Your love the answer to all things? Is that what You're telling me?" No. I'm telling you that the circuit, the complete and full relationship between us, is the very reason I created you. My love for you is My love through you. You achieve that circuit by your love for Me through the many steps you take as you grow spiritually in our relationship. It is not just that I bestow it; it is that we achieve it together.

If you look at the passage of your life, you might observe that you've made certain decisions along the way. Some of them have been bad. You've made some mistakes. But I'm grateful when I see you now because I know that you've made some very clear decisions to go with Me step by step. And it's through everything along your path—even those rocky times—that you've learned My heart for you; at least you've made steps in that direction. As you learn of Me and then look out at your family, at your friends, at the world, you begin to know My heart for everyone, don't you? And who can convey that? It's you.

My love for you is My love through you. We have worked to achieve that together. We will continue working this way until such time as the flow can be absolutely pure and full—your conscious relationship with Me and your conscious choice each day to allow My love to flow through you to this world. *You* achieved it! You achieved it by the decisions you have made, the path you have chosen in your life. I emphasize that you are not some robot I have made through which to express My love. It's our conscious cooperation together that interests Me. This is My goal for every life. There is no greater goal.

The sure path is to be open to the consciousness of the love of God—to allow yourself to become the flow of God's love into the world. I can't be the sole miracle worker; we have to achieve the miracles together. For this purpose alone I labor to be with you day by day as you become conscious of Me. I am concerned not only that you are happy, not only that you may experience My love for you and your love for Me, but that finally My heart and your heart become one. In that union My love can be fully expressed through your life—to your children, to the people around you, to the world at large.

Whatever you will bring—whatever uniqueness and gifts you have and whatever path you take in terms of who you truly are as an individual—will express that quality, that love. This is the real beauty that I intended to put on this earth through humankind and to spread throughout Creation.

When you look at the world today, it may not appear that this is happening. Yet I'm planting seeds everywhere. Be looking for them! Whenever you see a sprout, water it and rejoice, because the desert will one day come up green. There's a prophecy in the Bible: "In the days of the Kingdom, the desert will blossom as the rose." There are even people who are looking for trees on the Sahara Desert as a sign of the coming of the Kingdom of God. The real desert, however, has been the lack of this flow of living water through My people—even religious people who are going through their lives like little children, wanting this, wanting that, and who are expecting Me to do miracles. That's not the way to bring green to the desert; green is the new life of our maturing relationship.

Continue on the path of learning to know My heart for you. You'll discover more and more as we go along. As you look out to those around you, you'll increasingly feel this heart. My love for you is ultimately My love through you.

I am within; I have nothing but the desire to express My love through your life. We must take this path together. Great things can happen as your love for Me and My love for you become one. It's so simple—though not so easy to put into a few words. Be assured, however, that as you move closer and closer into relationship with Me you will discover how really simple it is.

15

Shopping Malls and the Poor in Spirit

Look into your heart and examine the patterns you follow in seeking self-fulfillment. What is it you do that keeps us separated? What can you do to come to Me with an open heart?

YOU, Takeko and David, have been saying how touched you have been by people in desperate situations, so greatly in need of solutions, who nevertheless just hold on and push their problems down inside themselves. Often those problems are so obvious to you, yet they try to hide them, fearful of revealing anything to others. They don't want to even admit they have a problem.

As parents you watch your children hold on to unresolved problems as well, yearning to get answers yet afraid to express what is bothering them. Perhaps unable to trust you, their parents, they pretend that nothing is happening, that everything is OK. When you see this happening, you may feel like saying, "Come on, we're here! Please open up to us." Yet they simply cannot.

Many of you hunger in your hearts to have that meaningful connection with your Divine Parent. You wish you could have direct communication with God but do not allow yourself to have it. You feel a real hunger to really know. You may even believe that God is there and that you have every reason to be loved and accepted just as you are and thus to have a personal connection with God. But somehow you still are not confident that this is possible.

All this is important to look at, and because it is so important I want to share with you a few concepts to explain My relationship with each of you. Of course each of you is different. Some of you really have discovered the key in your relationship with Me; however, many are still wandering in the desert. There's a passage in the Bible that says, "Blessed are the poor in spirit: for theirs is the kingdom of heaven." That has been a riddle for many people, because it seems to say that poverty is a good thing. But let's look at this a little closer.

It is through the spirit that our connection can take place—in the very heart of your spirit, that most holy place. But in your world, many of you were born and have grown up with countless things in your lives that are not of God. You grow so far out of touch with your own deep emotional and spiritual selves and with the things that would make for your development of these areas.

Life can become for you an endless string of diversions. Sometimes the things you collect have to do with worldly success—prestigious education and jobs, fancy cars, big houses, expensive clothes and jewelry. These can divert your attention from any sense of need for the Divine. But other things, such as failed relationships between spouses, parents and children, siblings, or close friends, can leave you deeply scarred, disappointed, and fearful of risking any kind of relationship with other people or with Me. And as life continues from childhood on up to adulthood, you become surrounded by more and more things that you have gathered in an effort to satisfy some inner longing you cannot quite identify.

Consider yourself. You were born into the world without even one piece of clothing. But look around your house and chances are pretty good that it is filled with more objects than you even know you possess. I know you think you need many of the things that you've gathered around you. But when you leave this world will you take even one of those things with you? No. You see?

On a spiritual or invisible level, you are a collector too. As you come into earthly maturity, you collect so many things, and good or bad, they occupy you. Maybe you know people who spend their days virtually obsessed with a job, hobby, or activity. For your neighbor, it is taking care of her yard—pruning and grooming and watering and fertilizing each little bush and plant and every blade of grass, seeking to make it absolutely perfect in her own eyes. But one day she will lie down and not get up again, and she will not take one blade of grass with her.

Even in the spiritual realm, until she realizes that this is not where real fulfillment lies, she may create the same sort of activity she had on Earth. One day gardening will pass away, and your neighbor will start to look for other things until she realizes that genuine fulfillment comes in a very clear, simple, and true relationship with Me, and thus with herself.

Everyone is looking for fulfillment of their spiritual essence, but people substitute many things for our relationship—which is the only place where they will find this fulfillment. And in a world that has fallen away from Me, some of the paths people take in search of their fulfillment are not only unhealthy but extremely destructive and, yes, even evil. How tragic that some seek their fulfillment by killing other people! They have to go out and make war and kill or rape or hurt others or do something that will destroy themselves or the Earth's environment in the name of fulfilling some appetite which they cannot understand. This is tragic!

Yet even in this warped extreme you see how desperately people are seeking to fulfill themselves, to find something that will calm that appetite, even when they've become so twisted in life. This is not true fulfillment that will calm their appetites, however, and this quickly becomes apparent. Their appetite can never be calmed until we come back together, until little by little they realize that what they are doing and the way they are seeking to fulfill themselves will not work.

The poor in spirit are people who see that they need Me and don't hesitate to reach out to Me. They are no longer fooled by false occupations or needs. The "rich in spirit" are those who are self-satisfied, those who have filled their lives with their own treasures. The poor in spirit see that without the Divine, their hearts—the castles of their spirits—are empty, that in essence they have no genuine spiritual life.

Do you know how happy I am whenever one of you reaches out to Me with your questions, your reflections, and even your pain? Do you know how that kind of trust touches Me? The poor in spirit reach out in these ways. Instead of saying, "I'm not worthy to communicate with my Divine Parent. I think I'll go shopping instead," they reach out. How many hundreds of millions of people choose to go shopping instead of making connection with Me their way of life? They go out to the malls and buy things they do not need and that only lead them to further anxiety and frustration. The shopping malls have made billions of dollars serving "needs" that are false substitutions for a relationship with Me and the true Self.

Even in the faith of the Christian New Testament there's a great need for Christ. Why? Because people feel they are sinners, that they cannot come to Me on their own. But if indeed there is to be a Kingdom, people must learn to come to Me. No, there will be no sinners here—but let Me remind you that *sin* means separation from God, nothing more. The Kingdom is a place of union with Me. And when is that day of the Kingdom to come? Who will initiate it? It will come from each and every one of you recognizing that you need God and having the willingness to approach Me directly from within your own heart.

Those of you who are parents know how sad and painful it can be when you see that one of your children needs to talk with you but will not come to you and ask. Part of you may want to shout, to reach out and pull them down on the couch so that the two of you might share. But another part of you knows that this moment cannot be forced, that the child's heart must be ready. This is what I feel when I look at My children. These children, in quiet desperation, are wandering around in the shopping malls of their lives and seeking what can never satisfy them instead of simply sitting down to share with Me.

Many people in the world are not even aware of Me, as you know. That is profoundly painful for Me. But equally painful is the realization that there are those of you whose religious beliefs and understandings immerse you in feelings of your own unworthiness, in the sense that you are not good enough to come to Me on your own. And there are also those of you who fill your lives with "good" activities, who serve your communities in the name of saving the world, yet you do not come to Me directly in your own lives. Some religious people may appear rich in spirit—giving out, giving out, giving out—yet you do not come to Me directly because you do not feel you are good enough.

"The road to Hell is paved with good intentions," it has been said. David and Takeko, you spent much of your lives helping other people, counseling and teaching and giving sermons. You spent many late nights on the telephone helping those in need. You were constantly reaching out. You finally came to realize that this activity was partially motivated by your own desperate need. So I say, reach inward to Me. This is the moment I wait for, and I'm saddened when I see people running around and seeking to save the world in My name yet not taking the time to reach inward to Me.

I want each and every one of you to reach inward to Me, no matter where you are. Recognize that you are always worthy in My eyes, no matter where you may be in life. Let yourself come to Me, poor in spirit, for then you are open and can become a conduit for boundless Love.

I know that in reading these talks, in seeking out My Word, you are reaching toward Me, seeking to find the way to Me. But do not forget that these talks are not an end in themselves. The real source, the real connection, is found in your heart. If these talks help to inspire you, if they became a conduit to your heart, then they have served a purpose. Yet it is only in your own relationship with Me that your hunger will be satisfied.

In a family, when a brother or sister comes into a room and sees a sibling talking with Mom and Dad, and love is filling the room, then that brother or sister quietly reflects how much they would like to be the recipient of that love. Or perhaps you are walking in a park and see two lovers talking so intimately that they don't even notice anyone around them, and you may think, "Wow, I wish I would have a relationship like that someday."

There's a loneliness, a sadness that you may feel when you see the love expressed through these relationships. And anytime that you feel this way, look into your heart and examine the patterns you follow in seeking self-fulfillment. What is it you do that keeps us separated? What can you do to come to Me with an open heart?

Be assured that you are not the only one who has your own shopping mall where you go in an effort to fill your inner needs. But there's an eternal shopping mall that we can visit together. It is called the Love Mall, the Heart Mall. Bring everybody there.

Know that I am here and that I will never go away as long as I know that you have this need for our connection inside of you. You may not even recognize it, but I do. I know. Don't stop reaching!

16

The Sunshine beyond the Rain

Free yourself of negative attachments! See them clearly through My eyes, from the inside out, and through the eyes of your higher self.

AS YOU continue to make significant steps going to different and higher levels in your unfolding spirituality, you may find yourself reassessing what your life has been about in the past. This process brings you into the deeper meaning of repentance, for *repentance* means *a change of direction*.

Theological perspectives, especially in Western traditions, rarely understand repentance, believing that it involves simply being sorry for a past mistake. This kind of remorse may be a component of repentance, but there is a deeper level of understanding that I would like to discuss. Simply being sorry for a mistake never guarantees that the mistake won't be repeated: You do something, you feel sorry or guilty, you repent. But feelings come and go, and in another situation your emotions will again dictate that same pattern of behavior you just regretted. Again you'll be faced with that moment of sorrow or guilt when you repent, and in time that feeling will pass and you'll find yourself making the same mistake again. This can go on and on throughout your entire life unless you understand the deeper meaning of repentance.

To simply make mistakes, feel bad about them, and repent, only to repeat the same cycle again, is the cyclical pattern you call "addiction." Addiction does not merely involve drugs, alcohol, eating, sex, or all the other addictions you find listed under support groups in the telephone book. Rather, addiction is a pattern of behavior in life.

I must say that My human family has been addicted to lower levels of consciousness. You won't find support groups for this addiction in the phone book because it is of a different dimension. It is causal, involving the entire pattern of one's living and being. And this lower consciousness is cyclical, manifesting through the generations.

All manner of addiction starts with a lack of a higher vision, a higher understanding, a higher level of being, or a higher vibration, if you will. And all of you who are attached to the lower levels of consciousness will remain in your addictions until you begin to see the higher level that is your spiritual potential.

Any time you come to realize another step ahead, you begin to hear the inspiration that comes from Me. You struggle to bring these inspirations into your daily life as real actions. But as you move to higher levels, you inevitably look back and see much more clearly all those things that cannot go with you to this higher level of living your life which you are now pursuing. And so you are faced with a difficult question: Do you want to stay with those old ways of being, or do you want to take the steps necessary to leave those ways behind?

As strange as it may sound, many of you are very attached to your addictions. It's like the "bag people" you see on the street with their shopping carts full of things that look like they should be thrown away immediately: a collection of buttons, stale food, dirty clothing, old newspapers tied together with string. As you look you may think, "That's disgusting. They should just throw that junk away." But you can become very attached to useless things, whether junk or a fancy car. Even if it is something as lowly as a bag of buttons, you would probably meet with great resistance if you tried to take it away. What you cling to has meaning for you even though no one else can understand it.

When I look out and see My sons and daughters, I lament, "How could these who are of My family be so attached to something so absolutely unimportant?!" You see, humans must devote themselves to something. And if you cannot make steps ahead, you will seek attachments and addictions that are of a lower level. But these are very poor substitutes for the higher path you yearn for.

Learn to recognize when you have become addicted to certain mental and emotional patterns that exist in your memory bank. Recognize that they are more than just memories you hold in your mind; they are patterns of emotion as well, encapsulated in the very cells of your body. They need to be left behind forever, yet this is not easy to do when you have been living in the realm of these memories, giving them life all these years, and even receiving and passing them along from one generation to the next. I know that you may feel you are caught between the desire to separate from these lower levels of consciousness, to say good-bye to them forever, and the realization that certain parts of your identity—perhaps more than you would like to admit—are wrapped up in them.

This is what you face as you come onto that higher path. And it will happen more than once because this matter of cleansing, of leaving your bags of buttons and useless trash behind, is not just a one-day or one-week or one-time task. There are many dimensions of your being, so developing a different self-image is a process of working through many layers of your identity. Many layers must be lifted away before you can fully recognize and realize your higher self, that place within you which directly interfaces with Me.

Free yourself of negative attachments! See them clearly through My eyes, from the inside out, and through the eyes of your higher self. As you do, you will more clearly understand what you must do. This is the time to recognize the addiction that has possessed humanity and that has possessed you. So today, even while many people speak of peace on the earth, the conflicts are becoming more clearly defined within each person, within families and tribes, and throughout the world.

People are about to become more aware. In the meantime, they will feel more powerfully than ever the anger, fear, sadness, loneliness, depression, and sense of futility to which they are attached. They will awaken to these patterns not because they are becoming more deeply ensnared by them but because their inner eye is seeing them clearly for the first time.

Think of it like this: You are walking in a rainstorm when, looking ahead, you suddenly see clear, bright blue sky. In the countless days preceding, the weather was gray every day. You became used to the gloom and didn't notice anything unusual. But seeing from the new perspective of the blue sky, you suddenly acutely feel the wetness and coldness of that constant rain. And this is what I mean when I say that you are experiencing your feelings more sharply: You are sensing more keenly the burden of your various pieces of old baggage.

You're still in the rain, but please don't simply sit down in it. You need to continue to walk; it's so important that you keep walking. Don't allow yourself to be caught sitting in the rain. Recognize that the baggage you are dragging along is not you. It's just what you have picked up as you have gone along—like the street people—thinking that you need it to survive. But carrying this baggage is barely survival! It is survival in a very dismal and unreal dream. I encourage you not to be caught up by these matters.

As you read these words, look at your own situation, particularly at those times when you feel downcast. Are you aware of repetitive patterns that tend to frustrate you now more than in the past? Realize that it is not only your old patterns of being which are frustrating you but that what matters most is that you are now seeing the blue sky. There is a greater hope now, a greater purpose to be achieved in your life. It is time to walk forward.

If you ask Me how to do that, I will tell you that part of the pattern which has kept you from going forward involves your fears of what you might discover in opening your heart. Also, you live in a world where the innocence that accompanies an openness of heart is looked upon with skepticism at best; you may even be criticized as being naive or stupid for opening your heart. But it is important now to be open in your life. After thousands of years of human evolution, look at what you have attained as a people. I simply ask you: Is this what you want? Life is far more miraculous than what you have known! You are being asked to open your heart. If your heart is not open, there can be no magic that will change your life, that will help you to a higher level. Not even the most enlightened soul outside you can help you if your heart is not open. This is a crucial point. It is you yourself who must go beyond your fear, go beyond those old patterns, no matter how much they might want to persist. See them for what they are. Discover the innocence that can be yours and let it be a way to fully open to communication between you and Me.

I love to hear your open-hearted communication with Me when there is nothing standing between us, even if for but a moment each day—no veils, no masks, no protocols. In these wonderful moments I can help you to open your heart even more and help you to move ever higher.

Learn from one another. Many of you are inspired in different ways, and I encourage you to learn from one another. Your own individual path is the only one you can actually walk, of course; you can't walk another person's path. But you can learn from others and they can learn from you. Your heart will tell you which person can teach you and which person you can teach. Listen to your heart and you will see.

My love is unconditional, and when you find that unconditional quality in others, be open to it. You will see it coming more and more through various people around you. Don't think that you are the only one having these experiences, for truly I am opening many hearts. Please go beyond the dismal rains that come into your life, the storms of the heart, and move on to higher ground.

It is of no concern to Me whether or not you feel inspired or uplifted when you want to communicate with Me. I don't expect you to come to Me every time like a happy little being full of light. Each of you will pass through many kinds of internal weather, and as long as you do not allow your fear to stop you, you can learn from every one of those states of being.

You can learn to leave your useless baggage behind by opening to Me even in those moments of deep depression, sadness, or undefined heaviness that you experience within yourself. Be open to Me in each moment. Bit by bit I can help you separate yourself from that which you carry, and soon you will leave your baggage behind. Please let Me show you.

17

The Importance of Our Sharing Everything

I hear everything—not only your words but also your heart as well as everything that you are experiencing at this time. Believe Me, I wish that I, by Myself, could instantly make everything better for you in every way.

Takeko: "Those of you who read these talks may wonder how we open our sessions with Heavenly Father. We don't usually record this part of these sessions in our writings, but I would like to describe to you what happened as it influenced the message we received today.

"We always begin with a simple meditation. We close our eyes, sometimes in silence, or one of us may feel a desire to express our heart directly to God. However, at times our everyday lives may interrupt this process. For example, this morning I had a great deal of pain in my legs, and I couldn't get beyond that physical pain to focus my heart and mind into meditation. I was frustrated, saddened, and angry.

"The physical pain triggered thoughts of other things that have been bothering me, like our family's financial situation and having to work so many hours to earn money that I haven't the time or energy to do much of anything else. My desire has been to work more directly on things that excite me, like translating these talks into Japanese. But time is passing and I haven't been able to spend the long hours needed for translation. My feelings of frustration suddenly came to a head.

"Yet I felt I couldn't bring these things to God. Somewhere in my mind I thought I had been bringing all things to God. I'm an honest person, and I want always to express what's in my mind and heart before God. But I find myself caught between total honesty before God and the ethic of my background which insists that you should never bother your parents with bad news.

"In my Japanese upbringing, I was taught to be a good child in front of parents and elders, to compose myself, to maintain a good posture, so to speak. My father was authoritarian, and I was afraid he would scold or reject me if I were to tell him my problems. So I learned how to become a "good daughter." As a young adult, I joined a church where I always had a leader. Once again I was encouraged to take responsibility for any of my own problems and not to burden others with my bad news. Although I told myself I was honest with others, deep inside I was frustrated because I couldn't really express myself from my gut.

"And so this morning my heart was racing. Instead of going into meditation and trying to find a very calm place to receive God, a lot of sadness, frustration, and anger started piling up. Above all, a lot of tears had to come out. I couldn't hold them back any longer. When we finished the meditation, David was calmly sitting next to me, and we wanted to have the usual sharing before Heavenly Father begins to speak. All I could think of were these things that were racing around in my mind, so I just expressed them. The following is Heavenly Father's response."

MY DAUGHTER, I gratefully receive what you have shared with Me this morning. I hear everything—not only your words but also your heart as well as everything that you are experiencing at this time. Believe Me, I wish that I, by Myself, could instantly make everything better for you in every way. I know that not only you but many other people in various kinds of pain (physical, mental, or spiritual) expect that somehow something will happen to change everything. Yet I also know that it doesn't always happen as you would wish.

I feel the suffering you feel. You may think that because I am almighty and divine that I'm somehow above it all as you, My sons and daughters, are going through your painful situations. But please remember that we are one family. One. With all My heart, I wish I could solve the problems you are facing in a single moment, but I cannot.

You know the story of Moses and the chosen people and their trial upon the desert? That is to be understood not only in the literal sense but on a deep personal level as well. The Kingdom of Heaven, that Canaan of comfort and joy, is not only a place to go in terms of external blessing but is also a place within you. You are still wandering out in the desert until you can learn certain lessons in life.

There are many kinds of deserts that people are wandering on. I know that many of you find yourselves wondering if there is some reason why you have to stay on the desert so long. You wonder whether you have made so many mistakes that you are being punished. You wonder when you can go into your promised land.

There is a point in every journey when you are faced with crossing a River Jordan, passing from your own desert into a realm of grace and liberation. This experience is unique for each person. Your recognition of that point is important. It is not something anyone can tell you, even if their heart is totally open to you. The best way for Me to work with you is directly, not through another person. For this reason, Takeko, I deeply appreciate that you were able to share openly and honestly with Me this morning.

My relationship with each of you begins with the kind of sharing that we have had this morning; be assured that I want you to continue to come to Me as you have done this morning. This may not be easy for you to understand at this moment, but the more you can pour everything out to Me, as you would with your dearest friend, the more I can help you.

Believe Me, I know that your path is made very difficult by your physical pain. You call it a curse. I know it is not easy to just go into prayer or a place of silence to meet Me, because the pain is like a dog almost constantly trying to attack and pull you. For this I am very sorry. I recognize that discouragement can set in, but please don't become discouraged.

Just as you have done in the past, many people think they must come to Me with only good news. They do not want to inconvenience Me with their burdens. They won't admit their need, guilt, anger, and frustration. Yet what is a true relationship between a parent and a child? You were frustrated as a child because you had to make yourself a certain way with your father. You had to hold back so much, and your anger built up until finally you shouted at him, defending yourself and your brothers and sisters.

That image of parenthood isn't Me—indeed, it has nothing to do with our relationship. I want you to bring everything to Me.

To do so is not unfaithful or disloyal. On the contrary, sharing with Me in this way is clear and honest and true. I am disappointed if you try to do public relations with Me in your prayers, if you try to show Me only what you believe is positive and respectful. You don't do this to be cheap or dishonest, I know. In your hearts you believe this is the way our relationship must be conducted, but unknowingly you continue to try to hide so much from Me. And like a spill in the refrigerator that you don't clean up, it becomes moldy and rotten, affecting everything around it. Understand that when you cannot express everything from your deepest heart to Me, it limits what we can do together.

Give up the part of you which still clings to that image of your childhood and your father. I have nothing to do with that. I want to help one hundred percent. And My direct relationship with you is what I treasure most of all. It is not just these Friday morning sessions with the three of us that are important. Far beyond these sessions and beyond any inspirational message I might offer you during them, what is most important is the constant, intimate relationship between us. We can travel many miles together in that realm beyond the physical, for the dimensions of your heart are so far beyond any words that come through in special moments or through a spiritual teacher or mediator.

I can help you most in this way. And we help one another—I don't know if you realize it or not, but by opening up and receiving My offer, you can also help Me. I too have been frustrated, because I have wanted to communicate with you. I have seen many times that the emptiness of My children—that is, the obstacles you put between yourselves and Me—limits our relationship. So My frustration is very much like yours.

When I hear your prayers and watch how you repeat the very actions that limit you and that create barriers to our relationship, I wonder, "Is it always the same thing, over and over again? How long does this have to go on?" I don't have physical legs in pain as you do, Takeko, but in a certain way your pain is indeed My pain. And so it's a very close thing between us.

I want all of you to know the power of our direct relationship. While spiritual teachers may be helpful up to a point, no matter how great they may be, they can never substitute for your one-on-one relationship with Me. Where I want to go with you is more and more deeply within your own self.

You don't have to take a lot of time during the week or set aside what you're doing. Don't think that you must separate your relationship with Me from the demands of your daily physical life. I am with you completely, always. I don't want to lose you. And I don't want to be distant from you.

One of the great riddles in life—and a very serious one—has to do with why you are asked to push and push to your extreme. You wonder when it will all come to an end. I hope you can understand Me when I say that there is a reality which each person must face, a point at which you will be required to give something up. What each of you may be asked to surrender will be different, but usually it will be the thing that most troubles you.

You are asked to put your troubles in My hand. Being able to do this is a great achievement, one of the most challenging you will ever face. It is one thing to abstractly say, "I have faith." It is quite another to put your most painful situation in My hand. Turn it over to Me so completely and unequivocally that you no longer have any attachment to it whatsoever, not even one fingertip on it. And continue to consciously place it in My hands day after day. This is where true faith is born and is tempered and proven. The moment that you gain the victory of surrendering to Me is when I can be most helpful to you.

I recognize that handing your troubles over to Me is not easy. There is a part of each of you that wants to keep holding on to those things which are most painful to you—your greatest test, so to speak, your greatest burden. Yes, it is difficult to face the vulnerability of putting everything in My hands. You may fear that I will do nothing. You may think it irresponsible to pass the buck to Me. I may not pay attention to you. I may be incapable of helping you. Or worse, you may have the impression that I *want* you to suffer tragedy. But this is not how it is.

I ask you, please, go beyond your perceptions of everyday reality. Turn your troubles over to Me. See if I am capable. This is not irresponsibility on your part. It is truly your entrance into Canaan. But I know that your passage through this gate is not an easy one.

I don't take the questions you have raised here lightly. And for all who might read these words—and I hope there will be many who will take these questions into their hearts—don't think that what I'm trying to give you through these talks are only the work of Takeko or David, because that's not so. I don't like being given personal lectures any more than you do. Meet directly with Me whenever and however you can. I want so much to reach out. Again, I ask of you to please share everything with Me, whether it be physical suffering, financial troubles, or difficult relationships. Don't limit your effort to reach out to Me to simply reading or studying talks such as these. I long for direct connection with each and every one of you.

18

The Intermingling of Heart in Daily Life

In relationships, the sum of one plus one is much bigger than two. It's a coming together in a deeper sense. It's a one-ness that is vastly richer and greater than you might imagine.

I WANT to start this talk with some thoughts about you, Takeko and David, because something that happened between us some months ago could serve as a wonderful object lesson both for you and for others who might read these words. I was reminded of the morning when you two had a very stormy argument. Your hearts weren't at all together, but when you became conscious of Me, we could suddenly share very deeply in what became excellent communication between us. This morning, while there is no argument, there is not so much talk between the two of you. So, hoping that others might learn through what we share here this morning, I want to take this time to discuss with you about making room for the other person in your thoughts.

In this world there are few true friends—that is, people who in their hearts can recognize what you value most deeply. You'll find people you can talk to and share with up to a point, but to find a true and special friend is like finding a diamond.

It would seem that, after living together for many years, any husband and wife should have the special bond of true friendship. But this is not necessarily so. To be able to share most deeply together is not just automatic to marriage, even though day and night, year after year, you may live together.

Friendship is rare, even in marriage. Long after the hot romance has cooled and after the children are grown, some marriages just barely hold together. Sometimes they hold together only because parents don't want to hurt their children by separating. Sometimes they hold together because the spouses don't see any alternative but to stay together. Or perhaps they even hold together because of religious or cultural fears. But are these not poor ways to conduct a marriage relationship?

Building true friendship within your marriage, Takeko and David, is critical in this world. That's why I've asked that before I come and speak with you, you two take the time to share. Whether you are expecting anything from Me or not, you need to take time to connect with each other and just share—not always about financial problems or this or that external obligation, but just share what's in your hearts. That's important, because in doing that, more and more you'll come to appreciate one another and what you're building together.

In relationships, the sum of one plus one is much bigger than two. It's a coming together in a deeper sense. It's a one-ness that is vastly richer and greater than you might imagine. That's truly the bond of a relationship. In the spiritual realm, the eternal world, you do not have physical bodies; you have the intermingling of your hearts. And while this intermingling could begin in your present life here on Earth, it is far too rare in this world today.

One of the real demons of modern culture is television—not just because of the programming but because it has pulled people away from sharing deeply with one another. At an earlier time in history, many families sat together in the evenings sharing their experiences—father to mother, parents to children, mother to father, children to parents. There is no greater treasure than the daily life and experience of the individual. Family sharing of this kind is still part of some people's lives, but it has become rare indeed. When it does take place, what a beautiful thing it is!

When many people go on to the spiritual world, they look back and feel very lonely. Why? Because they are meant to take with them into the spiritual world not memories about television shows but feelings for those they really mingled with in the deepest sense of heart. For those of you who have spent your lives trying to live out a godly purpose, this is a question that you will have to face long after the shoes of your earthly mission have worn out.

The question with which you should enter your older years is this: Who really knows me and whom do I know? Who really embraces me and whom do I embrace—beyond any ups and downs, beyond anything? This is so very important in the Kingdom of Heaven. Many people don't realize this. They think that everything in the Kingdom of Heaven will be covered by God and by God's representatives. But truly, it's not just glory coming from above; there is to be glory in each and every life. It's the glory of life itself, of really coming to a consciousness of the shared experience of life with your family and those around you. It's being able to mingle in heart, fully and deeply.

All I ever wanted was a family. In a big family living together in a big house, sure, there may be arguments and struggles, especially among the little ones, but the most beautiful thing in a family is the sharing and the intimacy that goes on, and not only between husband and wife, not only of a physical or a romantic nature, but truly on all levels and in all moments. What prevails is a feeling of being able to be free with those around you—totally free.

I know it is not easy for loved ones to find the time when they can sit down and really share what is in their hearts. Because of the tension of daily life and the struggles of modern living, I know that this is not easy for you or anyone else. But please realize that these times which you spend with Me are also times which you spend with each other. As your Father and Mother, that's My concern.

When you look at religion in the larger sense, there are people who are willing to give up their lives, who will bravely proclaim their willingness to die for God and their spiritual masters. But oftentimes these same people have become cold to their families, to the persons who are closest to them, as well as to the people right around them who are claiming to share the same faith.

A proclamation is not enough to establish the Kingdom. Throughout history, those who were willing to give their lives for Me would oftentimes turn around and brutalize their brothers or sisters in the worst way. Theirs is an incomplete understanding.

I do not ask only that you love Me or that you and I form a deep bond or relationship but that in your everyday life you reach out to others, from the deepest part of yourself, to express the love which you want to offer to Me. This liberates Me because I work through the heart and the network of love. This is how the Kingdom will blossom and thrive.

Consider this: When you read these words and share them with someone close to you, they in turn will share them with other people that they know. What I say here will eventually reach out to people all over the world. This is one strand in the network of the heart that I am telling you about. It is not just for those people individually to have a wonderful realization of Me or of the eternal things in their lives, but ultimately it is to bring people together to where you share your hearts and deepest desires.

You can come together and express the kinship in the family of God. Don't you feel this as you and others share what we are discussing and thinking about here? Yes, we are building a network in so many ways and in so many places—wherever there is an open heart. My work has come a long way, down through all of human history. Reaching far beyond all the lectures presented by all the various religions, I work in millions and millions of ways that are unknown to you. The future of your world depends on the network I have been building and on how well the spirit of God can flow amongst you.

There has been much suffering in the past caused by hatred and prejudice—and there continues to be suffering in the present. This will come to an end! But there must be something already building to swallow up that hatred and melt away that prejudice and that separateness which has tarnished all of human history.

While the words and visions offered by some religions can help provide road signs to the Kingdom, words and visions must eventually convert to experience and action for each individual. This comes down to each and every one of you gaining an awareness of Me and out of this taking an action.

As you become aware, the day-by-day path will not necessarily be an easy one, even within your own relationship and family. You may see many complications in your life, many things that appear to be demanding all of your attention and pulling you away from yourself and from Me. These demands and temptations must be met head-on. However glorious the vision, whatever the great hope, making these a reality is a challenge. And that is the challenge now before you and all of history.

I am certainly not looking for more "isms" in the world, for more and better doctrines. Much has been given. Now is the time when the training and development of each individual heart is necessary for bringing consciousness of Me into reality through each of you in your own individual way.

People have believed many things over the centuries. But belief alone is easy because it doesn't demand responsibility. You can say you believe in God, but what does that mean in terms of your daily life? How does your belief translate into your relationships with others or with how you regard yourself? Do your beliefs shape the choices you make? Do they convert to actions that benefit others as well as yourself?

Many have spoken of ethics and morals, but again, oftentimes those standards are not reflected in your everyday life. You believe that people should behave a certain way, but even those who have expressed very powerful beliefs in a certain moral and ethical structure have still fallen down and created a mess in their own lives and in the lives of others. It is not enough to have strong beliefs or strong convictions alone. It is so important that you learn how to enter the realm of the heart.

Why is it necessary to come into the realm of the heart? Because the heart deals with the here and now—this moment, not a day next week or a period of time long in the past. It deals with this moment because your heart is where you meet Me, and I am real only in this moment. I am not real tomorrow or yesterday; I'm either a hope or a memory, perhaps, but it is in *this* moment that you must live, taking this most immediate step on your journey. And if there is a hole in front of you, you must see it clearly.

Self-control and responsibility are important, because it is through these that you realize your daily relationship with Me. It is here, in your moment-by-moment relationship with Me, connecting through your deepest heart, that you can go beyond yourself and begin to take control of a life that is otherwise pushed and blown around by many storms, large and small. This is what I'm calling for, and this requires a lot from you.

Many people are seeking easy answers. For example, in Christianity it is easy to say, "Since Jesus died for my sins, I've been forgiven and so I'm going to Heaven." That is such an easy answer. But what about your life, the thirty, forty, fifty, sixty, seventy, or more years you have to spend in your physical body? Does the concept that Jesus died for your sins release you from any responsibility during all those years?

If anything, exemplary or sacrificial acts such as that of Jesus call for greater responsibility in living your life. The key to living in the here and now lies in the experience of forgiveness. Little children feel joy at their parents' forgiveness, even as they go out and make more mistakes. But as you mature into a truly great soul, you realize the power of forgiveness to release you from the bondage of the past—no matter what your transgressions may have been—so that you can live in the present moment.

When you, David and Takeko, came to Me several years ago, you experienced a deep sense of forgiveness, even without My speaking of it. You realized that I knew all which had passed before in your lives. Yet you came to know that My focus was not on condemning or criticizing or in any way belittling you but that I wanted you to go forward, to forgive your past and make something with you that was true and real and profound. And that remains our purpose here. It is our daily path together.

Just as with David and Takeko, I ask each who reads these words to really work on these things. Don't be afraid to open your heart more fully to Me day by day, even in the most mundane activities. Remember that I am always here. I am with you. And if you have the One who is your True Friend with you, then you can go through anything. That's what will give your life meaning.

Up or down, good or bad, when you carry with you that heart connection with which you feel our special link, you can face it all. And so it is with our relationship—and with the help of your relationships with others—that we accomplish these things.

In your day-to-day lives, try to remain conscious of My relationship with you. You will get caught up in many outer responsibilities, and it will be easy to put aside our relationship, to say, "Oh well, this is not the time for it." But this is not the way. Be assured that it is not a matter of becoming passive and just sitting around meditating. You can bring your relationship with Me into any and all activities in your life. Bringing the inner into the outer will give your life great meaning and proportion.

Whoever you may be and whatever your walk in life, I ask you to examine your marriage, your family, your friendships, your own heart. What is your pattern? What is your daily way of life? And if you call out to Me and proclaim your absolute willingness to give your life for Me, then I ask you to begin in your relationship with the person next to you.

Make a place for Me in all your relationships and with everything that you do.

19

The Mighty Stream from Heaven

The riches and the wealth that I have invested in each of you from the moment of your conception, from the very beginning of eternity, are beyond your understanding.

TAKEKO, I wonder if you would share the experiencc you had yesterday with your son.

> *Takeko*: "I went shopping with our son, who is graduating from the university. His graduation is such a special occasion, not only for him but for us as well. After so many years his student life is ending, and he will be leaving our home, beginning his marriage, looking for a job, and getting on with his life.
>
> "As his parents, David and I wanted to acknowledge this special moment and give our son everything we could. Some parents were giving a car or money or even more, but all we could offer was a pair of eyeglasses, which he needed; this was to be our graduation gift.
>
> "My son and I went to five stores searching for the right pair. The frames he had his heart set on were very

expensive, and we could offer only half of the amount. Having gone from shop to shop to shop and then having only enough money to pay half of the cost brought me to tears. I had wanted to give so much, and I couldn't even give one whole gift.

"With tears I told him I couldn't even cover the whole cost of his graduation gift. He said, 'Oh, Mom, I'm very happy to have what you can give. It's OK. I'm sorry, too, that I can't help you more.' I tried to hide my tears, but I wept all the way home.

"This started me thinking about Your situation with us—how You want to give us the whole world, how You are passionately ready to give everything to Your children. I was crying about one graduation gift and whether or not I can put food on the table tomorrow, but look at the number of your children who are starving right now throughout the world. Sharing with You, I said, 'Look, I cry just for the gift I'm unable to give my son. It was a bittersweet experience, but Your situation is that so many of Your children can't even eat or have roofs over their heads. How much Your heart is yearning when You see them starving and unable to recognize or reach out to You!'"

There are so many things I would like to say today, but if I told you what is truly in My heart I would go on forever. Your experience yesterday, Takeko, is very much My experience, the experience of not being able to give My children everything, of seeing their need and yet feeling that same poverty which you experienced with your son. There is such a poverty of understanding of Me in the world, even among those who have faith in Me and believe that I am the richest, greatest Father and Mother of all—their faith is still the faith of little children.

If you were to truly look around yourselves, you would ask questions like, "If God is so great and good, so wealthy in blessings, why is there such pain everywhere in the world? In every city, every town, there is hunger and physical suffering. Even more so, there is vast poverty in human relations, a poverty of love in the world. If God is so prosperous, so loving, and so good, why do we have all this poverty?"

As parents, you both desire to give absolutely everything to your children, to fulfill all their wants and needs. My situation, however, is uniquely different from yours. You do not at this time have the funds to give, while I am the wealthiest of all parents, ready to give but not embodied in this moment. I have been wandering and looking for the person wherein I can embody Myself, invest Myself one hundred percent through a human being. You are My children, and I long to be completely one with you, yet there is still such separation.

That heart which you felt yesterday, Takeko, is exactly My heart. Where is the breakdown? Where does this poverty occur between Me and you, between the Divine and the world as it is? The breakdown is in the realm of the human heart.

Millions of people pray every day that they can be blessed with a new car, a new home, better food on the table; they pray that I can give them a better life in the material sense. They pray for better relationships in their personal lives and for greater happiness. But however much I want to see that Myself, the channel through which I can work is the human heart. The human heart is the conduit into My infinite divine heart.

Your heart is your unique expression of My heart. Until you have connected with My heart and found that place within your own, and until those around you have also found Me in their hearts, all that I want to give you from My infinite love remains unexpressed.

A billion times a day in this world, people walk away from the deep impulse in themselves to express love, to reach out, to offer that love to someone in their life. For whatever reason, that impulse is often ignored, whether it be toward a husband, a wife, a child, a friend, or someone in need. The reason could be pride or fear or just habit. There are millions of reasons why people walk away from that impulse to love, to reach out, to do what their deepest heart wants to do.

On a far more serious level, there are those who are no longer even in touch with this impulse to love, whose lives have been scarred by alienation, hatred, and pain. Consider a nation of people who are at war with their own countrymen, where two groups of people are so alienated from one another, so hateful, that one killing another is like you killing a mosquito—like killing something tormenting you for which you have no feeling whatsoever. But we are talking about human beings here! That is My son or daughter being killed by My son or daughter!

You can't begin to imagine how I feel when one son aims a gun at his brother's head, pulls the trigger, and walks away as if he were just finishing target practice. This is the extreme of being totally unaware of the impulse to love and instead being overwhelmed by the impulse to hate. Am I in that human heart? Am I in the heart of one who holds a gun to another's head and pulls the trigger? Am I in the heart of one whose head is blown off by another of My sons? Yes, I am! Sadly, I remain locked in the prison of both hearts.

I am also imprisoned in the life of one who is not ready to love, who does not follow that impulse and puts it off until tomorrow. Maybe you can say that is a minimum-security prison, but unfortunately I am locked there too.

These talks are sometimes painful for Me because they are like letters from a prison. You, David, spoke about the letter that Martin Luther King Jr. wrote from the Birmingham jail, addressing ministers throughout America. This was a famous letter. It reached many people, touched them, and started a powerful movement to support the struggle for civil rights. I understand and applaud King's efforts, but My purpose and My joy is not in writing letters; it is in helping you to be in touch with what is in your own heart—in each of your hearts.

The prison for Me, the thing that has left this world in poverty, is that I have been locked into so many human hearts. This world is like one great prison, and thus the almighty, all-powerful, omnipotent, omnipresent God is not free. I want to be free! I don't want to write letters.

Holy books are a pain for Me, not because they aren't precious, not because they aren't true, not because the words aren't full of love and compassion for My people, but because I long to live through holy lives, in holy men and women who are open to Me and to one another, in hearts that follow the impulse to love. When you follow the impulse to love and give from your heart, you're blowing the door off this prison within the heart and allowing Me to come out.

I empathize with your feeling this morning, Takeko, because what I can give depends on what you can give. What I can express in this world depends on what you are able to express. I don't just work abstractly through so-called spiritual experiences. The greatest miracle of all is the presence that I have in and through your heart as it is fully liberated. For Me to be still imprisoned in your heart is as if you had ten billion dollars in the bank but by some terrible administrative mistake had no way to get to it. The bank has locked you out in the belief that you are an impostor. You say, "But I have no food for my children! Couldn't I get just a hundred dollars?" And the answer is, "No, not possible."

The riches and the wealth that I have invested in each of you from the moment of your conception, from the very beginning of eternity, are beyond your understanding. These are the riches and the wealth that will fill My Kingdom. That is why I don't like to work through letters and other stilted or abstract methods of communication with you. I long to work directly so that we can be as one, so that the unique riches in your heart, which are far more than an impulse, can be liberated to the world and pour out to all of My children like a mighty stream coming from Heaven.

Look at the way I am understood and you will see the poverty. Look at the way so many people—even religious people—understand their relationship with Me today. They seek Me in places where they will not find Me, not because I am not there but because they do not allow themselves to find Me. I want to see all of you graduate to something different.

I am not totally imprisoned by any heart, no matter how much one might deny My presence or be driven by hatred. Even when such a person seems completely closed to Me, I am still able to express Myself for their benefit and to give to him. But there is so much more that I wish to do! So please understand Me and know My heart as it is for each and every one of you. The greatest thing you can give to Me is an opportunity to live through you. Like Martin Luther King Jr., I am then released from the jail and am able to give in the fullest sense of the word.

You who read this talk, realize that I'm not just interested in having you study what is said here. I want you to know Me in your own precious life. I want to emerge fully from your heart. What you learn from that experience will be far deeper, far more powerful, and so much more subtle than anything these pages could offer to you.

I know that My investment in your life is constantly maturing. This is the era when a light such as yours can shine on this Earth. Don't doubt it! I am not speaking just to make you or other people feel good or to give empty spiritual statements. The key is your heart. Follow that impulse to do good and to love. It is, indeed, a mighty and creative stream from Heaven that longs to be released through you.

20

The Parental Challenge of Communication

Did you ever sit down and really talk with Me? If you would take that moment, you would find that the deepest and truest desires in your own heart are a reflection of My deepest and truest desires for you.

I WISH to talk today about the maturation of the heart.

With youth come great hopes and high ideals. This springtime of life is a time of powerful development, discovery, expansiveness, and looking forward. These are beautiful assets, characterized by high energy as well as strength, power, and vision, to encourage and motivate young people as they learn and mature.

As you reflect back on your own youth, you may do so with the perspective of the experience of your years and see those things which were lacking in your life at that time. Some may still be lacking, of course, and certainly it can be invaluable to look at these as well.

It is important to talk about the maturation of heart, because in youth one very often does not grasp the meaning and the depth of heart. It's often only in adulthood and older age that one begins to recognize the depth and fullness of this realm. In matters of heart, much conflict can be aroused between parents and their children because of the disparity between youth and the greater maturity that comes with age.

Parents are often concerned about their children's development of heart. Yet oftentimes the children don't seem to see this as important at all. They only want to break loose, get out into the world, and have their freedom. With this freedom, they feel, they can do what they want. They can set to work establishing what they think is right in their own lives and in the society around them. In some cases, they may have high religious or social ideals charged by youthful zeal aimed at changing the world.

The role of parents, meanwhile, is to guide the ship of the family—to steer the course. Parents are forever destined to worry about what their children are doing, sometimes even feeling hurt as their children take off at warp speed across dangerous waters. The parents see the boulders just under the surface of which the child is not yet aware. The child may race toward hazardous regions even as the frightened parent tries his or her best to warn the child about what's coming up. But the child, thinking that mom and dad just worry too much, fails to heed their warnings, which many times leads to sad or painful consequences.

First, the child doesn't seem to listen. Second, the child can be injured emotionally, spiritually, or physically by the very circumstances the parents warned him about. Third, it's extremely difficult for the child to come back to the parents and admit they were right all along. A million variations on this theme occur every day between parents and children.

Many of you reading these words have experienced this kind of thing over and over again. The question is how can you communicate, how can you help your high-energy, idealistic child to see what you see and to take in the knowledge that you have already collected in your life? It cannot be helpful if you simply speak out to the child in a way that makes him feel condemned for what he's doing. I know you don't feel this way in your own heart of hearts, but you want to strongly impress on him the point that you feel, so you may pepper your comments with dire warnings or even remarks which seem to the child that you are judging him or her. Then the question is how to reach him, how to let her begin to be aware of the meaning and value of what you are sharing? How do you express yourself so that your thoughts can get to his heart?

David, I speak to you now, but My words will apply to thousands of others. In your youth you were a high-energy idealist who charged ahead, racing toward those rocky places and dangerous waters that I knew were there. You didn't listen to Me very much. Very few young people in history have truly made a sincere effort to hear Me. It's only in later life, or sometimes in difficult or serious circumstances, that you will turn to Me.

In my position as Parent, I see everything. I see far more than any parent in history ever could, because I am the warp and the weft, the whole weave of reality. I know everything in terms of the possibilities for your life, both constructive and destructive, yet I am listened to very little. Yes, it is painful for Me, too. I'm called great things such as almighty, omnipotent, omnipresent, but still it deeply hurts Me when My children don't take the time to listen and when you don't trust that I have your best interests in mind. I'm trying not to limit you in the warnings and direction I offer but to show you a place where you need not limit yourself.

Even with God, communication is a two-way thing. However complete My wisdom, if you to whom I'm trying to speak are not open to listen, then the results will be anything but perfect. And then you walk away perhaps completely unconscious of My own broken heart—only conscious that you goofed, blew it, failed. You might be angry and blame yourself or someone else for that failure. You may even blame Me. Sadly, you did not truly open your heart and listen.

Until turmoil, difficulty, or tragedy came into your lives, few people in history have ever really listened. This is the source of My own suffering as a parent. My comforts are not like yours, in that I am not comforted by your bringing Me flowers or a cup of tea or attending to My every whim. Rather, I find My greatest comfort in sharing with you as parent and child, in simply finding someone who is open and can sit down to receive Me as I am. This is not easy to do because of all the preconceived notions about Me.

In regard to My relationship with you, let Me remind you that young people have many preconceived notions about who their parents are and what their lives are about. They think that their parents are old-fashioned and narrow-minded or that they simply don't understand. Today many people say that believing in God is old-fashioned and that God represents a repressive religious perspective. To such expressions I can only say, you don't know Me! Did you ever sit down and really talk with Me? If you would take that moment, you would find that the deepest and truest desires in your own heart are a reflection of My deepest and truest desires for you.

In your relationship with your children or with other young people around you, do you offer them moments when they can be open to your heart and truly know you as you are, free of any preconceptions? Such moments are not easy to catch. Perhaps in your mind, too, who I am is boxed up in an image that is completely wrong. Maybe you'll have to wade through many blockages, many assumptions, many feelings from your childhood and then put them behind you before you can truly see Me.

With you, David and Takeko, it was only in that moment after the accident that you became good listeners. I could finally share with you as I am. You found Me not to be wearing the nametag of any particular doctrine or religion. You found in Me simply a Parent who has only your best interests in mind, in the deepest sense—even far more than you do. Then we were able to communicate in the way that we both desire.

This is the way I long to reach each and every person on the face of the earth—not through tragedy but through an opening of the heart. This is a complex matter. You have five children; I have six billion. Indeed, looking at all the people who live on your planet, what will it take for My children to really speak to Me and listen to Me as I am? Let's not speak of any widespread tragedies. But were such tragedy to come, and with it an opening up between parents and children, then that tragedy would become a blessing.

In your own parental hearts, you pray that your children might be spared tragedy or heartbreak, yet you do not stop wishing for openings when you can sit down and share with them. You long to offer them the help of all your wisdom, your prayers, and your closeness to Me. Perhaps they will marry and have children of their own. Be sure to take time for all this, knowing that what you offer can have an impact on many generations to come.

Let's shift our attention slightly for a moment. When you see so fully and clearly what your children do not see, it seems obvious that they would want to hear what you have to say. After all, you have knowledge they don't yet have. Unfortunately, with the high energy and visionary or idealistic nature of youth, they may not want to listen to their elders. They want to find out for themselves. They say, "That's what you found, but I want to do my own finding."

It takes great tact and love to introduce the wisdom which you have gleaned from your years of experience in such a way that your children can be open to it. Look at Socrates, a man of great wisdom. How did he teach? He went about the streets asking questions. He tried to motivate people to draw out of themselves those ideas and realizations that he couldn't discuss with them more directly. He drew from them insights and understandings that he knew they possessed within themselves.

This is your challenge as parents and as educators of your own children. There are times when you will need to speak straight and strong because you may be revealing a disaster that can still be averted. But there are also times when, even though you know you are right, you cannot just put out what you know. You must help them open their eyes so they can see what you see rather than just telling them what you see. Even then the decisions will be in their hands. Yes, I know it's not easy for you. I faced all of these circumstances with you and with all the generations before you billions of times over.

I am amused by the Hollywood portrayal of Me. They gave Me that wonderful voice of Charlton Heston, and I always speak with absolute authority: "You must do this; you must do that; go here; go there." I wish it were that easy. Perhaps I should turn my job over to Charlton Heston! Yes, sometimes I boom out, but often I speak with a very small voice. Sometimes I ask questions, like Socrates. Sometimes I remain silent, knowing that only your own experience will communicate the truth you require.

Relationships are not a simple matter, even for God in My kinship with humanity. People were not made to just follow directions; I made each of you with your own path of self-discovery. As you discover the world around you, you truly discover yourself and who you are. Bringing someone to that discovery, helping that person see and take those steps, is an infinitely deep and subtle process.

I urge you as you labor with your children to take the time to carefully consider all that I have said here. I know it can help. I speak from experience; My experience with you is what I draw from. I will be with you as you share with your young ones, but for now it is time to close.

21

Transitions

The root of your spiritual development is your relationship with Me, not your ability to cling to a set of beliefs!

THIS morning you have spread a large banquet before us, a banquet of issues, stories, and many lives. Yet there is a common theme that runs through all of them, stringing them together like a necklace. This theme is transition—the changing of one thing to another.

In nature, transitions are very much a way of life. Seeds from a tree in the northern climates may migrate to hotter climates and in the process of growing to maturity develop a different kind of bark. Animals that live in the southern climates will have less fur than their cousins of the same species to the north. And you see transitions in growth patterns from year to year. A tree shaped one way this year will sprout new branches and look different next year. Nature adapts to its surroundings. Is this good or bad? It's not a matter of good or bad but a matter of learning to live with change. Everything is always changing and growing.

People sometimes ask if humanity is an exception to this rule. No, it is not. Your body, your life in the physical realm, is constantly in transition. Tremendous organic, cellular intelligence exists within you, and enormous changes are going on in your body all the time, allowing you to grow, to adapt to the climate around you, and to fight off infections and impurities that come to you through your mouth, your nose, or your skin. From childhood to maturity, your body must constantly adapt, and at the same time it is growing in size and in experience.

When I speak of humans, as you know very well, I don't speak only of your physical existence. I speak also of the eternal equation of your mind, your emotions, your spirit. In each of these areas and in all of them together, growth constantly occurs. At the most simple level of the child's growth, the desire for knowledge is fundamental. Watch young children around you and pay attention to what they say and do. Everything in their life is, "What is this? What is that? Why is this doing that? What did you do? What is this little animal that you have in the cage? Why does he do that?" They are constantly wanting to know, wanting to know. And as children grow, they are finding particular interests and really focusing on understanding all that they can in one area or another. Perhaps one child will become interested in helping people who are sick or hurt, and she will turn to medicine in her life. If she's great in that, maybe she will decide to become a brain surgeon. Perhaps she'll even pioneer new realms in that field. The desire to understand more, to know, is a beautiful thing.

Your spirit is like this. It is the very center, the very essence of human life. Your spirit was created with the same insatiable curiosity as that of your mind. Your spirit wants to know; it wants to grow. It has a deep nature within it that wants to breathe in the essence of everything in Creation—both of the physical world and of the spiritual realms as well. The spirit can be inspired by beautiful physical vistas such as an amazing mountain scene or a misty ocean coast. But in essence, what inspires the spirit is the beauty and majesty conveyed through the mountains or through the ocean.

In their spirits, humans have the capacity to perceive dimensions far beyond the physical realm. In the beauty and power of the physical realm, something is conveyed to you that makes you want to create; the greatest of paintings, the greatest of poetry, convey something beyond just the physical lesson—something far beyond.

When people visit the Sistine Chapel in Rome, they are overwhelmed by what the artist Michelangelo created. They are so touched by this creation that they often cry. Why? Because something is conveyed in the paintings on those walls and ceiling that is far beyond the paint, far beyond just the physical creation. The artist's spirit expresses the presence of God, the sense of holiness, power, goodness, and light that he himself felt. The visitor to this place is moved in spirit and touched emotionally. There is a majesty expressed that brings tears to the eyes of even those who have no religious beliefs. This is the beauty of the human spirit. It wants to drink up, to eat up all of that meaning, all of that power.

What is the purpose of such beauty? Where does it lead the human spirit? Let's go back to the example of the child who develops an interest in medicine and becomes a fine brain surgeon. She operates on a thirty-five-year-old person with a brain tumor and restores him to perfect health. But you know what? In another fifty or sixty years, that brain is going to die, no matter what you do. So it's not unlike repairing a tire on your car. A mechanic might do a beautiful job on your tire, but in another twenty or thirty thousand miles the beautiful job that he did will be forgotten; the tire will wear thin and will one day be discarded and replaced by a new one.

Thus, in strictly physical terms, this brilliant surgeon's wonderful skills cannot bear eternal fruits. They can only restore that patient's health for the course of his natural life, whatever that might be. But spirit touches the eternal. Great spiritual growth, accomplishment, and knowledge—the fullness of spiritual love and beauty—are eternal. And what is your destination? What is your eternal goal? I created you to be an ageless and unique reflection of My own nature. For that reason, your spirit constantly seeks Me.

Again we come back to this point of growth and continuous development—transition, as you would say. In its essence, transition is not just a process of moving along and finally reaching a specific destination; rather, it is a continuous process of changing from one thing to another, to another, to another, to another, to another. It is continuous movement. All people and all things have that nature of transition—continuous growth and development.

I want to bring your attention to a common historical human trait that has often hindered your destiny. Whether in philosophy or religion or science, people try to put a flag at a certain point and say, "Now we have reached this pinnacle and there is no further destination." And then you gather around that flag and say, "This is where we're going to stay because this is the truth with a capital T!" But finally someone else comes along and says, "Yes, I understand that this point where you put the flag was a very significant point in the transition of humanity, but look—the development is continuing."

When this occurs, many times you do not recognize the need of transition, the ongoing nature of growth and development. In fact, many of you will fight to proclaim that you need go no further, that you have discovered the ultimate truth and that any effort to change it would be blasphemous. And so the flag that yesterday represented a great new moment for Me and for My children may today become an impediment. To understand this requires an openness and a profound respect for the nature of transition.

You may become troubled by such statements and say, "If change is constant, then I can't believe in anything. If I try to believe in something but tomorrow brings further change, what good is it? How can we ever find anything approaching stability in our lives?" Let me remind you that belief is not the root of spiritual development. I've told you this as many times as we have met. The root of your spiritual development is your relationship with Me, not your ability to cling to a set of beliefs!

Let us go back for a moment and consider human life before what you call the Fall, that is, before humans had any sense of being separate from Me. During that time, your relationship with Me was central, as natural to you as it is to the plants and animals around you. And day by day, out of that relationship came a very natural development where change simply was a fact of everyday life.

I ask you, "What did you believe then?" Did you stand outside the flow of change and development? You might have looked very strangely at anyone who asked you, "What do you believe in?" You might have answered, "What do you mean? It's not a matter of what I believe in; it just matters that this is what I am. What I am living in is natural growth. It's my being."

If you walk up to a tree in your backyard and ask, "Well, what do you believe in to grow as you have grown?" the tree, were it capable of speech, might look at you and say, "Huh? What do you mean what do I believe in? This is the way I am. This is the way I live. It's not a matter of what I believe. It's simply who I am."

You could say, "Of course, that belief is a result of what you are." But unfortunately, since the separation, My people turn things around backwards: First they believe, and then out of that belief they try to become something. But this is not necessary.

You need not believe to be. "I Am that I Am," I told Moses. It is the same with My children. And out of that Being—that I-Am-ness, if you will, that very natural state of relationship between you and Me—comes your values and your beliefs. First the Being, and then the values and the beliefs.

So many times My people get confused on this point. This usually occurs because people become fearful about taking the right path. One of the dangers of this backwards approach is that someone puts that proverbial flag in the ground, which represents their belief system, and says, "Believe in this!" And those who pledge their undying allegiance to that flag become stuck to that spot. Do you understand? And what is the flag? It is "God." It is "the Christ." It is "the Truth."

Now, those who would not stop but who would seek their own nature in their relationship with Me walk away. And then the person walking away from the flag is judged as ungodly by those still gathered around the flag. "He is leaving God!" the true believers say. Time and again, the great men and women in history, the pioneers and forward-thinking people—not only in the history of religion but in the scientific community and in every other place where people hold strongly to certain ideas or ideals—have had to endure tremendous suffering for their determination to live in transition, to grow and develop.

Ironically, that person who would continue to grow and develop may one day find a flag of his own and plant it. Then people will gather around him and once more repeat the same pattern. That's why you, David and Takeko, must never make a church of your talks with Me—planting your flag and judging people according to whether they agree with you or not. Live your lives day by day and be open in your hearts and minds to Me and to the world around you. There can be much grief and tragedy in planting a flag and judging others according to belief. History continues to reveal this in every corner of the world.

Look at your own family and your own life as you read these words. Chances are that you will see change all around you. Perhaps an older child is moving out of your home, or someone else is getting married, or someone is ill or recovering from an illness, or another is changing careers. Perhaps someone in your family or circle of friends is not quite sure of where she is going but needs to change. Another person in your life is holding to a way of life or a set of beliefs that you no longer follow, and there is growing tension between you as that person seeks to draw you back to the fold. Meanwhile, you may be exploring bold new territories. All of this is transition—the growth, the development, the constant becoming of spirit.

Stand back and look at the nature of transition throughout history. There are more personal kinds of transition as well. Take the young person's transition out of his family. Oftentimes there are many sparks, many emotions around young people beginning to stand on their own feet. Parents feel anxious that their children will make mistakes, and sometimes disagreements between child and parents ensue. There is great instability for the child around taking that position of independence as he or she leaves home. It's a stormy period at best. In a way, parents feel the need to plant a flag for the family, to say, "This is what you should recognize before you leave here." Transition is never simple.

Look at the history of your own family's handling of transition. In the transitions of your family, you will be called upon to be open to your children and other family members and friends as they make their transitions. Face your fears with them, acknowledging to yourself and to them that you are nervous about what's going to happen with them. I've faced the same situation with the whole of humanity. I see that your knowledge is far from complete, that there is still a lot of immaturity, yet I can't force you down a certain path. So I will simply be there for you day by day. And this is how parents and friends can best serve their loved ones in transition.

Know what it means to be there for others. It means that if they step into a deep hole they can call out to you and you will help them. But do not condemn them for stepping into that hole, even though you may have warned them about it. Through these moments you can come to new realizations. You can discover how to be truly helpful, and they may safely learn how to not step in that hole again. Becoming capable of this generosity of spirit is not easy for either friends or parents .

Spend quality time with your loved ones. There is no substitute for open communication. This doesn't mean that everyone will walk away feeling that their problems have been solved, but if you can each walk away feeling that there are people to turn to when you are going through a stormy period, you have given a gift that is priceless. In this way, even storms between you won't destroy your relationship, and they may even bring you closer. Though perceptions and beliefs may differ, and even though there are not clean, simple conclusions, open communication allows relationships to continue and the heart to mature.

And so it is in your relationship with Me. I am said to be all-knowing, all-understanding. But I know also that in your process of growth, particularly in light of the gifts I have bestowed upon you—free will, creativity, uniqueness, and the capacity for self-discovery—I can't just tell you everything and expect you to catch on. Your discovery will involve many painful moments as you reach into the beehive, so to speak, forgetting that along with the honey comes the sting.

I am with you always and in all ways. I am here because I want to be with you as you journey along your chosen paths. And I can help you through those difficult moments that come out of incomplete knowledge, incomplete development of the heart. I can serve as your grounding and your foundation.

Recognize that the many flags which you, humankind, have planted as the Truth, the Final Answer, are not the end of the quest but merely way stations on an ongoing, eternal path.

In closing, I leave you with a remark that may seem like a contradiction: I am unchanging; My love is forever unchanging. But upon the foundation of my unchanging Being we both can discover tremendous growth and development. Your life will be rich and powerful and wonderful when you come to understand how this works and finally see that there is no contradiction in Me after all.

22

Will You Come to Me Before or After?

Your growing and learning to be more worthy has never been a condition of My love for you and never will be. Come to Me, even with all the imperfections that cause you to beat yourself up.

MANY of My children stop themselves from coming to Me by clinging to thoughts or concerns that they are not worthy. But I want to be very clear about this: I do not judge you in this way. Worthiness and unworthiness simply do not exist for Me except that I see how these concepts trouble you.

You have known small children and have observed how rarely they are burdened by these adult ideas of worthiness and unworthiness. Imagine how you would feel, for example, if you were visiting the parents of little Diane and she refused to come and say hello to you because she felt that she was unworthy. Maybe she felt she was too childish, or she hadn't taken a bath, or her clothes weren't perfectly neat and beautiful, or she had talked back to her mother that morning, or she was feeling sad.

How would you feel if your little friend, who ordinarily delights you with her presence, was thinking she was unworthy of your love? What if she just hid away in her room while you and her mother finished your visit? If you are like most people you would feel a deep sadness for this child, and you'd probably feel disappointed or even hurt that she did not come to visit with you.

Most young children have very few concerns about their worthiness. They come bounding into the room with a runny nose, a dirty face, and messy hair and with absolute confidence and the desire to share with you any little thing that they want to talk about. That is the beauty of small children. They do not question their worth. And My longing for you is that you would come to Me as a child would—with confidence and no judgment about your own worthiness.

Picture in your mind, if you will, a criminal who has committed heinous acts against humanity, against Me, and against his own true self. Sentenced for thirty years to life, he is sitting in prison and has begun to think deeply about Me and about the life he has led. He begins to cry and calls out to Me; he comes with a heart that seeks only Me. Consider his small cell and the prison environment. It is not easy for him to work everything out in terms of his past, is it? He may have raped or even killed someone, but he just reaches out to Me. Regardless of how evil his life has been, whatever darkness has consumed him, he reaches out. Do you think that I don't hear that plea, that heart, that voice calling out? I not only hear, I answer! Think of how much greater his suffering would be if he were to sit there in his prison cell for the whole thirty years saying, "Before I can approach God I must become worthy. I have to work everything out."

Now let's imagine a person who has never committed a crime and has never knowingly harmed another soul. Let's say that this person is a devoted member of this or that faith. But she has learned a lot about the sins of her ancestors and is struggling to come to terms with her own past wrongdoings, however small these transgressions might have been. Imagine this person going through life thinking, "I'm not worthy of coming to God yet. I have to work this out. I have to get certain things straightened out. I have to wipe this nose, iron these clothes, study the Bible more diligently, and read all the books I own about my relationship with God." Unlike little Diane, who just comes bounding in, on and on she goes, making all these efforts to get herself in good enough shape to come to Me.

If this is your pattern, the chances are pretty good that you will never come to Me. I'll tell you why. First, think of that word *unworthy*—not worthy. When a little child comes to his parents, all that child knows is, "You're my mom and dad." And all of his mischievous activities of the day are forgotten. He just wants to embrace his parents, even if he has a runny nose or dirt on his clothes. That expression of love captures a parent's heart.

When, My son or daughter, however unworthy or valueless your actions have seemed in your own eyes, you suddenly realize that you need your Divine Parent more than anything in the world and you simply reach out, My heart is deeply moved. I am as moved by your reaching out to Me as I am by any of those who have struggled their whole lives to prepare themselves to be worthy. It is the reaching out that moves Me, not a person's efforts to conform to society's secular standards or religious standards or your own standards.

You see, when you return to our original and most truthful relationship, it is perhaps a bit like going back to babyhood. Babies make nothing but work for their parents. It's drudgery. Parents have to change diapers and clean bottoms, feed their babies, and wake up in the middle of the night when they cry. Do the baby's actions make it worthy of the parents' love? By some definitions of worthiness, the answer would be no. But worthy or not, the child instinctively just reaches out to the parents, emotionally and spiritually, and the parents' hearts are moved by the bonds they feel.

When you study the face of a baby as it gazes into its mother's eyes, what do you see? Joy, peace, and trust. That mother is the representative of the Divine for the baby. The baby has not yet learned how to judge and criticize itself. It doesn't say to itself, "I shouldn't have pooped in my diapers this morning. Now I am unworthy of my mother's love." And if the baby were to have such thoughts and thus feel unfit to gaze into its mother's eyes, you would have to conclude that it was a severely troubled baby.

Reflect on the part of yourself who has "pooped in his pants" many times. Suppose you are so worried about your past transgressions that you are convinced that you must completely master all your problems and somehow make amends before you can seriously consider even approaching your parents. For adults, this poop represents immature emotions, poor relationships, actions that have hurt yourselves or others, the development of bad habits, and so on. But all those poops—so-called sins and omissions—do not define who a person truly is, nor do they in any way affect My response when you reach out to Me.

Jesus said, "Unless you change and become like little children you will never enter the kingdom of heaven." What does this mean? It's just what I said: The little child has an innocent heart as he comes to his parents. Regardless of whatever mischief he may have gotten into, he has surety that these are his parents and that they love him.

I am saddened when I see you who have made great spiritual and personal efforts to clean up your lives yet who are still consumed by this sense of unworthiness. You are plagued by the desire to first clean up. Did you ever think that this is not an enlightened habit? Like alcoholism or smoking or any other bad habit, it needs to be seen for what it is. This is the ego's vicious circle, a bad habit of the mind and the emotions to paint a picture of My love that isn't true.

This bad habit can breed behavior that takes you farther from Me rather than closer: Outwardly you seem to be working very hard to come to the day when you will be worthy enough to approach My throne, while inwardly your original self is crying out to just come to Me. Tremendous fear and anger build up because of your inability to go beyond your ego. You feel confusion about why God doesn't just accept you—when it is not Me but your own ego who is telling you that you are unworthy. And you may think, "Why must I go through all these things before I can come to God?" Such frustrations become a powerful source of anger. But don't you see that if you put these judgments of your worthiness or unworthiness upon yourself, you are making your own presumption that I will not accept you just as you are? Who is telling you that you must work all these things out before you can come to Me? I can assure you that it isn't Me.

I hear the voice and the heart of the person who has been condemned to prison and who, in spite of his crimes and the dreadful life he has lived, opens his heart and reaches out to Me. Yes, I embrace that son or daughter. With tears I hear that voice.

I know there are many among you who have lived much of your lives with feelings that you are unimportant and unworthy. And maybe you even feel angry, wondering why God doesn't accept you and receive you. To all of you I say, "Do you see that I have been there for you all along, waiting for you to just reach out to Me?" Some of you, I know, must endure great suffering and even tragedy before you understand what I am telling you now. But this is not necessary, either.

Your growing and learning to be more worthy has never been a condition of My love for you and never will be. In the moment of your conception—and even before—our relationship was already defined. It is a parent-child bond of love, a bond that has never been broken and never can be broken.

Come to Me, even with all the imperfections that cause you to beat yourself up. None of these self-judgments determine your ability or inability to come to Me. All through history religious institutions have taught that you cannot make much of an impression on God until you have reached certain standards of achievement. But My love is not confined to any such conditions of these teachings.

I maintain our relationship from the moment of your conception. That relationship is the most fundamental thing in your life, and it matures and grows to encompass all. It is the basis of everything in your life. It saddens Me when you become totally occupied with the belief that before you come to Me you must do or be something different from what you are right now. Truly, spiritual growth is grounded in our relationship. Believing that you have to prove your worthiness before you can come to Me is a big ego trip!

In Western history, the one you call the Christ comes as a mediator, helping to mend your relationship with the God-from-Whom-humanity-fell-away. This is the teaching. But do you think that this Christ represents a distant God in some other part of the universe and that somehow if you buy a ticket from the Messiah then you can travel to visit his God? No. A messiah comes to remind you that God is within you. If you want to buy a ticket from that messiah, it's ultimately a ticket to your own heart.

I am saddened that so many people who follow Christ, in the West particularly, have failed to receive the teachings he brought. You accepted him and even accepted the ticket he offered you to make that shortest journey of all to God. But so often you didn't know which train to get on. You didn't know where to go. Where you are to go is right back to that original relationship with Me, and that is the relationship with your own Inner Throne, within your own heart—where I have always been. This is your birthright as a being created in divinity. It's not complicated at all. Just stop obsessing about your sins and imperfections and immaturities, and you will see it clearly.

The real beauty of all the holy men and women who have come to Me throughout human history is simply this—that they just came to Me. They all just called out and recognized that the fundamental groundwork for any meaning in life was this relationship with Me. You might say, "That was easy for these great spiritual leaders. They were not incomplete or imperfect like me. This person or that—be it Buddha or Jesus or Mohammed or Moses or any other holy person—was already perfect and worthy." But it was not worthiness that determined this connection with Me. It was the same for them as for you—an open heart that reaches out to Me. And yes, there were many who had to go through a lot before that moment of reaching out.

Let go of all the beliefs you may still be holding that you must somehow make yourself perfect and complete before coming to Me. You who are trying to exorcise all your demons before coming to Me, who are trying to erase all evil before you approach Me, realize that I am already in your heart. Once and for all, rid yourself of all thoughts of worthiness and unworthiness.

Your daily prayers, meditations, and disciplines are merely tokens to make the journey into your most inner heart and meet Me there. To bring you to this meeting place, which is the Kingdom, is the true purpose of all religion and spiritual training. Give up your beliefs that you must be complete and perfect before coming to Me. Come to Me in all your incompleteness, and you will begin to experience your completeness.

Many teachings have presented a picture of Me as a distant God living high on a mountain in a land far away. The truth is that I have always been right here within your heart! I close this talk with this reminder: Coming to Me is the shortest journey in the world.